BRIDGES FOR HEALING

BRIDGES FOR HEALING

Integrating Family Therapy and Psychopharmacology

Roy Resnikoff, M.D.

University of California, San Diego

BRUNNER-ROUTLEDGE
ALERE FLAMMAM
Taylor & Francis Group

USA	Publishing Office:	BRUNNER-ROUTLEDGE
		A member of the Taylor & Francis Group
		325 Chestnut Street
		Philadelphia, PA 19106
		Tel: (215) 625-8900
		Fax: (215) 625-2940
	Distribution Center:	BRUNNER-ROUTLEDGE
		A member of the Taylor & Francis Group
		7625 Empire Drive
		Florence, KY 41042
		Tel: 1-800-634-7064
		Fax: 1-800-248-4724
UK		BRUNNER-ROUTLEDGE
		A member of the Taylor & Francis Group
		27 Church Road
		Hove
		E. Sussex, BN3 2FA
		Tel.: +44 (0) 1273 207411
		Fax: +44 (0) 1273 205612

BRIDGES FOR HEALING: Integrating Family Therapy and Psychopharmacology

1 2 3 4 5 6 7 8 9 0

Printed by Sheridan Books—Braun Brumfield, Ann Arbor, MI, 2000.
Cover design by Ellen Seguin.

A CIP catalog record for this book is available from the British Library.
 ∞ The paper in this publication meets the requirements of the ANSI Standard Z39.48-1984 (Permanence of Paper).

Library of Congress Cataloging-in-Publication Data

Resnikoff, Roy.
     Bridges for healing: Integrating family therapy and psychopharmacology / Roy Resnikoff
       p. cm.
     Includes bibliographical references and index.
     ISBN 1-58391-050-6 (case: alk. paper)
     1. Family psychotherapy. 2. Psychopharmacology. I. Title
     RC488.5.R476   2000
     616.89'156—dc21   00-049368

ISBN 1-58391-050-6 (case)

To Jill Green, with love.

CONTENTS

ABOUT THE AUTHOR

Roy Resnikoff, M.D. is a clinical professor of psychiatry at the University of California, San Diego. He has had a private family psychiatry practice in La Jolla, California, since 1975. Dr. Resnikoff conducts training workshops on the integration of family therapy and psychopharmacology, and he is also on the faculty of the Gestalt Training Institute in San Diego. He received his medical degree from the Albert Einstein College of Medicine in New York and completed his psychiatry residency at the University of Colorado.

Photo by Lynn Saur at the La Jolla Cove.

FOREWORD

By Erving Polster, Ph.D.

Dr. Resnikoff offers a paradigm of psychotherapeutic practice and theory that illuminates the diversity of options available to the practitioner. This diversity invites practitioners to a new age of psychotherapeutic endeavor, breaking territorial boundaries that have confined them. In addressing these restrictive theories and practices, Dr. Resnikoff integrates two sets of theoretical vehicles that have been frequently polarized: psychopharmacology and psychotherapy, and family therapy and individual therapy. Resnikoff also shows therapists how to integrate instrumental and relational therapeutic styles and use both spiritual/communal and individuated perspectives.

These and other supposedly dichotomous approaches have often placed their adherents at war with each other, each side squandering the value offered by the other side. By merging these positions, Dr. Resnikoff has opened the range of therapeutic options, which benefits all therapists. The breadth he offers is both impressive and sorely needed in a field where practitioners have often allowed familiar theories to narrow their approaches. I believe we are ready for the breakthrough this book offers.

A major contribution is Dr. Resnikoff's attempt to take the mystique out of pharmacology, showing how it may be applied to individual situations and coordinated with psychotherapy. For a long time, therapists have believed that medication is a barrier to treatment, because with medication, the therapist is presumably no longer dealing with the "real" person. This altered version of the person would not be a fair representation of the patient, who would not be able to engage authentically. Dr. Resnikoff softens this view of medication, not only by describing medication's palliative effects in helping the patient through crisis, but also by showing how medication actually enhances many patients' openness to therapy. He not only offers his own work, but also introduces the reader to the already developed literature into which his views of pharmacology fit. Like people disenchanted with strict political ideologies who look for the practicality of political positions, people in the mental health fields are transcending ideologies to include innovations that work.

Included among these innovations is family therapy, still a fairly exotic intervention even though it has been around for at least 40 years. While having positive value, family therapy is still not as widely used as it should be. The reasons are unclear; perhaps the logistics of setting up sessions is a factor. But there is also a gap in the skills of practitioners. For example, many practitioners understand the importance of family therapy but lack the expertise to use it. And many who might value family therapy lack sufficient background to see its benefit in particular cases—or they may lack sufficient referral sources. Understanding the centrality of the family is as old as psychotherapy itself, but how to use it is, oddly, still confusing. Resnikoff helps make family therapy accessible to all those who understand the dynamics of the therapeutic process.

This book is a breath of fresh air from the center of therapy theory rather than its partisan edges. Readers of widely divergent theoretical positions will look to this material as a source for expanding the therapeutic repertoire. The writing style is clear, easy to read, instructional, and well organized. Resnikoff uses the literature to show the growth of interest in both family therapy and pharmacology. Though the book is geared to readers in the general field of mental health, it will also be of interest to readers outside the professional field who are part of the burgeoning concern with family and pharmacological issues.

PREFACE

During my 25 years as a clinician and teacher (including 9 years of presenting the family therapy review course at the psychiatry annual meetings), I have witnessed the pendulum in family therapy swing from directive problem-solving, symptom-focused modalities, on the one hand, to nondirective, "narrative," "object-relational," and "psychodynamic" conceptualizations, on the other. In the field of psychiatry, the pendulum has swung from an emphasis on psychosocial etiologies to a focus on biological and "cognitive/behavioral" approaches. In clinical practice, as well as in my role of teaching family therapy to psychiatry residents, the challenge of helping students develop a full repertoire of approaches has required me to synthesize the current psychiatric concepts with the family therapy concepts that have emerged in the past 35 years.

This book will help family practitioners of all disciplines, and families themselves, to integrate the long-standing professional and cultural dichotomy between relational and instrumental concepts of healing. By "relational," I mean spiritual, nondirective, empathic, and humanitarian approaches. By "instrumental," I mean behavioral, problem-solving, medical, and cognitive approaches. I will use dimensional concepts (that is, the idea of thinking along a spectrum or continuum) to help integrate the many approaches now available for helping families.

Within the field of family psychiatry, I will attempt to bridge the division between biological and interpersonal approaches. I believe that my unique contribution is the integration of psychopharmacology used in the "medical model," which targets symptoms and abnormal biochemical processes for change, with psychopharmacology used in the "relational model," which enhances communication and awareness of family issues.

"Family psychiatry seems split off from biological psychiatry," members of the family psychiatry caucus lamented when they met at a recent psychiatry national meeting. Family psychiatrists from various regions of the country noted that biological constructs and family systems' interpersonal constructs were on parallel tracks, rather than integrated in most psychiatry training programs. One participant pointed out that interpersonal factors were omitted in many psychiatric practice guidelines.

In the nonpsychiatric marriage and family therapy fields, organizations such as the American Association of Marriage and Family Therapists and the American Family Therapy Academy are thriving. Shelves at bookstores throughout the country are crowded with self-help books filled with pragmatic advice on how to parent, how to find a mate, how to relieve anxiety and depression in relationships, and how to make marriages last. Pop psych books proliferate on subjects ranging from deciphering the differing languages of men and women, to understanding long-term dynamics that might interfere with achieving intimacy, to achieving a sense of belonging and feeling loved. Radio talk shows offer advice on how to deal with interpersonal problems and are among the most listened-to shows on the air. Millions of Americans are apparently engaging in vicarious therapy during their daily commutes. But, overall, there is no clear direction in the field of marriage and family treatment.

This disarray seems true even though excellent summaries and books have been published in the past on the topic of competing constructs in marital and family therapy. My goal is to offer a model that integrates this information, providing clinicians with competing points of view so they can see the range of therapeutic possibilities in working with families. Lynn Hoffman, in her excellent book, *Foundations of Family Therapy* (Hoffman, 1981) and a 1990 *Family Process* article (Hoffman, 1990), described four main types of family therapy. She clarified the family therapy "lenses" that include systemic (process), structural (form), dynamic (historical), and existential (evolutionary) schools of thought. Hoffman, however, did not offer practical clinical guidelines on how to integrate these approaches; such guidelines will be offered throughout this book.

In his book, *The Body Speaks* (Griffith & Griffith, 1994), James Griffith sensitively illustrates how psychopharmacology can be used in family therapy and highlights the polarity between using psychopharmacology for treating diseases and using it for enhancing communication. Instead of promoting an integration, Griffith openly states his preference for narrative enhancement uses of medication rather than medical uses. Medical and humanistic pharmacotherapy will be integrated in the following pages.

Interestingly, the popular psychiatrist Peter Kramer has written books that on the one hand address the psychopharmacology of Prozac (Kramer, 1993), and on the other hand address marital therapy issues, such as whether couples should stay together or separate (Kramer, 1997). His work articulately illustrates the wide range of knowledge needed by the contemporary therapist, but lacks a plan for helping the clinician incorporate such far-ranging perspectives. I will be proposing such a plan. The work of Doug Breunlin, Richard Schwartz, and Betty MacKune-Karrer (1997), which outlines six "metaframeworks" for family therapy, and the work of William Pinsof (1995), who describes an integrated problem-focused therapy, will be reviewed in Chapter 1.

Because the assumptions underlying various types of family therapy are very different, the task of synthesis is complex. The medical model's biological approach defines disease states that account for depression, schizophrenia, obsessive-compulsive disease, attention deficit disorder, and bipolar illness. Based on this assumption, the family's role is to adapt, accommodate, or compensate for an individual's expression of such a disease. An opposing view holds that individual and family symptoms and problems are induced by system stresses and environmental changes that have, for example, compromised the immune system or induced reactive behaviors that provide metaphors, protection, and symbolic compensations for the systemic difficulties. A third major assumption identifies developmental difficulties or traumas that inhibit the normal progression and integration of personality or organizational factors, leading to later interpersonal difficulties.

A possible synthesis of these three viewpoints involves dialogues about biological versus environmental factors within each of the four stages of therapy. For example, although a medical disease state might exist, a family with strong organizational systems and coping styles may be able to override intrinsic biological difficulties. John Bowlby (1969) has pointed out that certain mothers with high bonding skills can override hyperactive temperaments in infants. In a more negative example of environment overriding biology, Bernice Rosman (Minuchin, Rosman, & Baker, 1978) points out in her pioneering work on psychosomatic families that dysfunctionally enmeshed families can make the treatment of diabetes or sickle cell anemia far more precarious by blocking treatment to avoid conflict. More recently, Jeffrey Schwartz (1995) elaborated on Lewis Baxter's work (Baxter, Phelps, & Mazziotta, 1987) documenting increased areas of brain metabolism in obsessive-compulsive disease. Schwartz found that although obsessive-compulsive illness appears to be a biological event mediated by the caudate nucleus, behavioral control alone, aided by the willpower of the client (and enhanced by family support), can reduce symptoms and change metabolism (PET) scans in the brain to a more normal level.

In pursuing an integrated family therapy approach for both clinical and teaching purposes, I have been influenced by Erv Polster and the philosophy of gestalt therapy. Gestalt therapy includes a basic awareness/clarification approach that, although emphasizing the present, has the potential to enhance openness to change; it also emphasizes contact and communication functions that are crucial for interpersonal work and mediation between differing points of view. Clinical flexibility can be promoted by gestalt therapy's shifting focus between background and foreground therapy issues, as well as by understanding and bridging the holistic polarities of surface symptoms within a biological and environmental context. Erving and Miriam Polster's dimensional integrative model (Polster & Polster, 1999) and Michael Solomon's conceptualization of family therapy stages (Solomon, 1973, 1977) will be outlined in Chapter 1. The Polsters' dimensional thinking and Solomon's stages form the framework for my approach to integrative work with families.

Chapter 1 presents an overview of integrative concepts, using as an example the family situation presented in Judith Guest's novel, *Ordinary People* (1987), which was made into a film directed by Robert Redford. The four stages of therapy are outlined as a sequence of therapeutic focus. Chapter 2 again gives an overview of the four stages, this time emphasizing the use of pharmacotherapy in each phase of family therapy. Chapters 3–6 each focus on one of the four stages. The description in Chapter 3 of a personal problem of the author illustrates how the professional pendulum shifts from psychodynamic models to biological models. It also illustrates the debates within many families between a biological, medical approach and a more relationship-oriented, humanistic approach. Chapter 4, using clinical examples, shows how the therapist can openly present basic theories and principles to the family in the spirit of experimentation rather than manipulation. Personality-oriented family therapy, which deals with the ways personalities mix, match, and develop in relationship to each other within a couple, marriage, or family, is the focus of Chapter 5. Chapter 6 focuses on how the universal or traumatic issues faced in a family's life transitions can be addressed with an integrative therapeutic approach. Paul Fleischman's 1990 work, integrating spirituality with psychotherapy, is reviewed and illustrated with clinical examples. Chapter 7 discusses the importance of supervision in integrating therapists' differing personality preferences and assumptions regarding the etiologies of mental illnesses. Competing professional influences on the therapist are also addressed. The supervision process is examined as a parallel process to family therapy, with the dimensions of family work similarly creating flexibility in the therapist. Chapter 8 includes a summary and synthesis for therapists dealing with the complexity of issues in family therapy.

My hope is that the dimensional model will become gradually more and more familiar throughout the book, empowering the therapist/reader to use and bridge the best of many clinical constructs for family healing and growth.

The clinical examples have been changed to protect the identity of the families presented.

Roy Resnikoff, M.D.

ACKNOWLEDGMENTS

I thank Erving and Miriam Polster for their encouragement and support over the last 25 years. Erving Polster's ability to encompass paradoxical concepts and methods is the inspiration for this book. I wish to thank Deborah Lapidus, my associate for 16 years. She has coauthored several articles with me, including an article that was the basis for Chapter 2; our clinical minds are in synchrony.

Lewis Judd and the Department of Psychiatry at the University of California, San Diego (especially Stephen Shuchter, Sid Zisook, Hagop Akiskal, and Stephen Stahl), have provided a fertile arena for me to learn contemporary psychopharmacology, alongside my role of teaching family therapy to psychiatry residents.

Bill Baak, Les Kadis, Ruth McClendon, David Janowsky, Norman Glenn, Jenny Mudge, Ira Glick, Mike Solomon, and Peter Manjos also deserve a word of special thanks. The Gestalt Training Institute of San Diego (Sharon Grodner, Rich Hycner, John Reis, Anna Walden, together with Erving and Miriam Polster) provided much needed professional support and encouragement.

To make a book like this possible requires extensive practical help. Mae Kavanagh spent endless hours typing and retyping. My brother, Neal Resnikoff, Kathleen Neumeyer, Deborah Lapidus, Jill Green, Jeff Jones, Fred Belinsky, and Patricia Fornes all contributed by making comments on the manuscript. Jean Femia helped with the final editing. Harold Sweet produced the graphics. The staff at Brunner-Routledge, especially Tim Julet, Katherine Mortimer, and Toby Wahl, encouraged me to have confidence in the project. Joel and Rosanne Holliday provided an ideal Montana retreat for writing; John Engel and Tom Sauer gave personal support in addition to legal advice. My sons, David and Alan, gave needed encouragement and support (there are some advantages to the "empty nest syndrome" in terms of having more time for this project).

Concepts of Family Therapy Integration

☐ Why Integration?

The last 20 years have seen an upsurge of interest in integration in both psychotherapy and family psychotherapy. Like the postmodern developments in art, literature, music, philosophy, and architecture, this interest in integration attempts to fuse and blend multiple influences, and it appears to be a response to increasingly polarized theories and methods in the field.

Contemporary debates have raged about the contribution of genetics versus the environment to homosexuality, language development, conduct disorders,

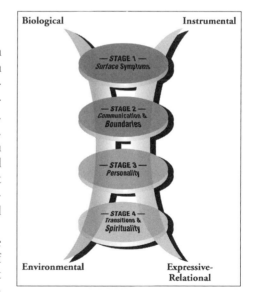

and personality disorders. The explosion of technical advances and the availability of psychopharmacology have prompted an opposite renewal of interest in spiritual, cultural, and gender issues.

The ongoing struggle between "foreground therapies" and "background therapies" has pitted an emphasis on problem-solving against an emphasis on historical patterns and other contextual concerns. Paralleling the societal trend toward fast food, managed care, and Internet retailing are similar efforts to simplify and abbreviate services to families, including providing help only for family surface symptoms and problems. In opposition to this trend are attempts to preserve interpersonal, humanistic approaches to therapy.

Turf wars between professional groups have polarized professionals and dissolved into political struggles. A backlash encouraging integration is one reaction to the splitting and competition between professional groups.

Jay Lebow (1997) points out the increasing popularity of many concepts—such as therapeutic alliance, loss, life cycle, cohesion, differentiation, rituals, engagement, resistance, and termination—which are universal to all schools of family therapy. Lebow explains integration as not only simply logical and a sign of the postmodern realization that any one method is limited, but also as a response to the pragmatic pressure of including everything that "works."

The author has been motivated to integrate various approaches to helping families for several reasons. First, as a therapist, to join a family and gain a therapeutic alliance, one must initially be concerned with foreground problems. But in most situations, to be truly effective, one must gradually move to background contextual issues such as communication problems, personality issues, and life stresses. Second, integrating therapies and methods means "having it all"—one can use the best of both the directive and nondirective approaches. There is, in a way, a triangular struggle to emulate both father-like gurus, who create rapid changes, and mother-like guides, who emphasize process and relation concepts leading toward general healing. Third, on a more spiritual or holistic level, one yearns to find meaning in one's work by connecting seemingly paradoxical elements of human style, experience, and therapy. One hopes to offer a relief from suffering, while also forming a connection with people and things, rather than being only a technician.

I believe that integrating all the prevailing approaches is clinically crucial for four reasons:

1. A therapist must combine some initial problem solving with exploration of background issues. Schools of family therapy promote differing theories: the problem is the problem, the family structure is the problem, personality difficulties are the problem, or life transitions and spiritual issues are the problem. The clinician needs a way to organize and apply all of these theories.
2. A therapist must understand contemporary advances in pharmacology

in order to benefit from psychopharmacology's clear effectiveness in controlling unwanted symptoms, as well as enhancing interpersonal connections.

3. A therapist must work within the current professional political framework and dichotomies of psychotherapy organizations. In professional turf wars, some groups insist on humanistic awareness, narratives, and empathy, while other groups insist on short-term behavioral, cognitive, or psychopharmacological problem solving. The therapist must integrate the best of these differences in working with families in order to enhance therapeutic options.

4. A therapist can increase effectiveness by incorporating traditional/historical methods and strategic/directive methods in an open, nondirective, respectful, and collaborative way, rather than disregarding such methods as "politically incorrect."

☐ The Four Dimensions

Dimensions for Integrating Family Therapy and Psychopharmacology

From my experience in psychiatry, family therapy, and gestalt therapy, I believe that four dimensions can help clinicians and families integrate a seemingly polarized and confusing set of viewpoints and guidelines. Each dimension is a spectrum or bridge between opposing positions. These four dimensions are:

1. Foreground versus background stages of therapy;
2. Instrumental versus expressive-relational methods;
3. Biological versus environmental causes;
4. Therapist versus family dimensional interaction.

The First Dimension: Foreground Versus Background Stages of Therapy

The first dimension is derived from the work of Solomon (1973, 1977). It involves the notion of how a "therapeutic alliance" is developed (that is, how the family and therapist begin to work cooperatively). His idea is that the therapist first joins the family with surface foreground issues and then gradually follows the process of family therapy into more complex background concerns.

Key questions for the therapist start with foreground issues and move to background issues during the four stages of therapy:

Stage 1: Surface issues

• What is the presenting problem of the family?
• How is the therapist selected?
• What are the surface symptoms?
• What is the sequence of events around the surface symptoms?

Stage 2: Communication and boundary issues

• What are the boundary and power issues in the family?
• What are the communication patterns in the family?

Stage 3: Personality issues

• What are the personality dynamics within the family?
• What are the personalities and personality polarities (opposite person-ality characteristics) over three or four generations in the family?
• How are the different styles and approaches within the family inte-grated?
• What are the couple/marriage personality characteristics and polarities, and how can they be integrated?

Stage 4: Transitional and spiritual issues

• What is the current developmental life-change issue for the family?
• What are the traumatic life challenges facing the family?
• What are the gender and cultural influences on the family?
• How are the family's spiritual needs met?

   This first dimension is especially helpful in integrating the various schools of family therapy that focus primarily on one stage (symptoms, boundaries, personality, transitional/spiritual) to the exclusion of others. Of course, the therapist constantly moves back and forth from foreground to background at each stage of therapy development. The developmental process of family therapy is seen as similar to human development, where simple functions are gradually expanded to relationships and to the world. In integrating the stages of therapy, the therapist and family decide what the foreground versus background issues are at each stage.
   Chapters 3–6 discuss in order the four stages of therapy.

The Second Dimension: Instrumental Versus Expressive-Relational Methods

Nondirective therapies emphasize the paradoxical theory of change— that awareness and clarification spontaneously lead to new behavior. In contrast, strategic and structural schools of family therapy, behavioral and cognitive therapy, and traditional pharmacotherapy all emphasize direct corrective change.

The change oriented, directive approaches I have labeled "instrumental." The nondirective, narrative, and psychodynamic approaches I have labeled "expressive-relational." How to incorporate the ends of this dimension will be discussed in relation to each stage of family work. Psychopharmacology can have both instrumental and expressive-relational benefit; integration is promoted by considering the entire dimension within the polarities of these two points of view.

The psychopharmacology expressive-relational emphasis of James Griffith (discussed in Chapter 2) is especially useful in helping families with psychosomatic disorders such as headaches (Griffith & Griffith, 1994). Griffith views pharmacotherapy not only as a change agent for target symptoms but also as an agent to facilitate the narration, awareness, and clarification of difficulties within the family before any changes are made.

The Third Dimension: Biological Versus Environmental Causes

The human potential movement in the 1960's emphasized that the family or individual can choose their own destiny. Over the last 10 years, the clinical emphasis along this dimension has shifted toward biological and genetic aspects of emotional disorders. There is a similar biological versus environmental etiology debate about cognitive development, sexual identity, delinquency, and personality development, and at every level of family therapeutic intervention.

In the third main dimension, biological, genetic, and organic dysfunction will be integrated with environmental and family dynamic factors to help understand family difficulties and, again, the potential use of psychopharmacology. This dimension will be considered at each stage of family work.

The Fourth Dimension: Therapist Versus Family Dimensional Interaction

A fourth main dimension is the therapist's interaction with the family. The therapist's ability to work along the foreground versus background, instrumental versus expressive-relational, and biological versus environmental dimensions will be discussed as both an internal process for the therapist and an interactional process with the treatment family. This dimension ranges from the family's self-support, with the therapist facilitating

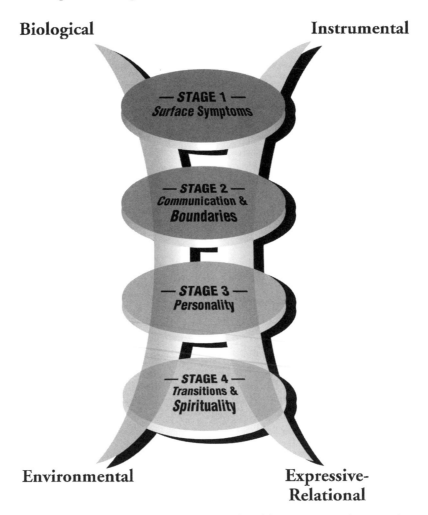

Biological   **Instrumental**

— STAGE 1 —
Surface Symptoms

— STAGE 2 —
Communication &
Boundaries

— STAGE 3 —
Personality

— STAGE 4 —
Transitions &
Spirituality

Environmental   **Expressive-
                                            Relational**

FIGURE 1.1. Four main dimensions are considered for integrating pharmacotherapy with family treatment: 1) Foreground versus background stages of therapy; 2) Instrumental versus expressive-relational methods (directive change versus nondirective clarification); 3) Biological versus environmental causes (nature versus nurture); 4) (represented by shadow) Therapist versus family dimensional interaction (therapist personal issues that resonate with family therapy treatment issues).

awareness and dialogues, to the use of the therapist as an external authority to create change or protect the family. Therapist supervision includes teaching flexibility regarding family self-support versus therapist support, with the degree of therapist activity and help being integrated with the family's self-help.

Using the Four Dimensions

These four dimensions (see Figure 1.1) can organize the various schools of family therapy together with psychopharmacology into a practical, clinically useful approach; they help summarize and simplify the many treatments available to clinicians. The ideal family therapy integration in clinical practice would be to have families and therapists alike understand all four dimensions and use their full ranges. The goal in helping families is not to be satisfied with just solving problems or increasing communications. The goal is to be able to flexibly use an integrated, internalized schema of approaches to guide families toward a sense of well-being and enhanced meaning.

The author hopes to provide a practical, clinically useful method for integrating the differing approaches for helping families as well as for helping families and therapists consider psychopharmacology.

☐ A Clinical Example: The Family in *Ordinary People*

The characters and situations in the 1981 film *Ordinary People* provide a timeless family therapy teaching example that will be used to give a practical overview of dimensional integration. Universal questions of loss, parenting disagreements, differing personality styles, and divorce will be addressed using the four dimensions (see Figure 1.2).

FOREGROUND versus BACKGROUND
Clinical Issues Dimension in *Ordinary People*

(1) **Surface Problem** – sequence around son's quitting swim team.
      Son decides → mother attacks → father defends

(2) **Boundaries Issues** – father and son against mother.

(3) **Personality** – Mother – narcissistic, blamer (villain)
      Father – dependent caretaker, placator (rescuer)
      Son – obsessive-compulsive, intellectualizer, depressive (victim)

(4) **Transitions/Spiritual Issues** – mourning process – death of elder son.

FIGURE 1.2.

Judith Guest's novel *Ordinary People*, adapted for the screen by Alvin Sargent and released in 1981, is the story of a family thrown into crisis after the death of a teenage boy in a boating accident. The mother and father seek counseling for their younger surviving son who has become suicidally depressed.

The mother had been closer to the deceased son and the father to the surviving son. Their personality styles were complementary, with the father's being more outgoing and flexible compared with his wife and surviving son, who both had obsessive thinking, rigid behavioral rituals, and were not directly expressive when it came to feelings of grief or anger. Interestingly, the opposite personalities in the family were paired, mother and lost son, father and surviving son, mother and father.

In the story, the surviving son receives successful individual therapy for his depression and learns to be more expressive. He receives electro-convulsive shock therapy to relieve a suicidal depression. Unfortunately, in the months after the death, the parents grow more apart, with the wife eventually leaving the marriage. The therapist is individually oriented, but does meet with the father, once, about the father's family system concerns. Many months after the death, the wife is invited to therapy, but refuses.

One basic way to organize and initiate clinical thinking is to take one relevant slice-of-life sequence of events, around the identified patient, for scrutiny. One such sequence takes 5 minutes, at the halfway point of the film. During this scene, the son, about 6 months after the death of his brother, indirectly informs the family that he is quitting the swim team. The mother responds narcissistically, claiming that she should have been notified directly. She also provokes guilt by saying that the son is embarrassing the family by announcing his decision publicly. The father, giving lip service that the son should "respect" his mother, defends the child, eventually saying that the mother is too harsh and selfish. His view is that the son needs support and compassion for his decision. The sequence also illustrates the ongoing alliances, with father and son joining—excluding the mother.

The clinical challenge here is to consider the four dimensions and the possible introduction of psychopharmacology in helping the adolescent and his family.

Paralleling the organization of this book, this clinical vignette will be discussed in the following order:

1. surface problems
2. communication and boundary issues
3. personality issues
4. life-transitional and life-stress issues
5. therapist issues.

At each stage, the therapist and the family would discuss instrumental versus expressional-relational methods and biological versus environmental preferences for addressing the issues of that stage.

Stage 1: Surface Problems

In an initial interview, the therapist would advise the family of the "multi-layered" nature of the therapy process, including organizational, personality, and transitional issues (foreground versus background issues). After general introductions and a detailed review of how the therapist was selected, specific problems would be addressed.

Instrumental Versus Expressive-Relational Methods

The initial problem-solving approach would be to clarify the teen's desire to quit the swim team and then to promote a family discussion regarding the pros and cons of this decision. The sequence of (1) the son acts, (2) the mother criticizes and feels victimized, (3) the father defends the son and attacks the mother, would then be explored. The therapeutic approach would be to clarify surface problems rather than initially curing or changing anything. This expressive-relational approach might lead to better negotiations and a well-considered decision spontaneously.

   At the more instrumental end of the spectrum, directed exercises with the parents taking alternating periods of guidance (Selvini-Palazzoli, Cecchin, Prata, & Boscolo, 1978; Tomm, 1987a) could reduce the vicious cycle of arguing. In directed communication dialogues, quitting the swim team could be considered both from a negative "dropout" point of view and as a positive statement of assertiveness regarding preferences. The therapist can also use storytelling that introduces a desired result (compared to stories told without strategic intent that demonstrate empathy and understanding of the family situation).

   Certainly a therapist would wonder initially whether the tension in the family is lingering from the recent death and resulting grief, but the therapist would follow the surface issues presented by the family with compassion and kindness until the contextual issues become foreground, perhaps openly stating this priority. ("I will be very interested in reviewing the family's reaction to the death, 6 months ago, but perhaps first, we should try to resolve this immediate swim team conflict.")

Biological Versus Environmental Causes

Especially when considering psychopharmacology, nature versus nurture explorations are needed. From a biological point of view, the living son was suicidally depressed after the brother's death. Normal grief can benefit from antidepressants even if it is not a "classical pathological depression." The question is whether the immediate swim team argument reveals the teenager still suffering from a biological grief or depressive reaction, leading toward depressive "dropping out" thoughts. An antidepressant might help in this medical model (Shuchter, Downs, & Zisook, 1996).

An alternate view, worthy of family discussions, would find the marital stress and personality conflicts, together with normal grief, sufficient to explain the swim team argument. Without medication, the therapy could proceed through stages 2–4 after the dropout decision is made. The son could easily be seen as having recovered from his depression with clear preferences and assertive language, and not needing medication.

Usually while exploring surface issues, other contextual concerns including organizational problems, contact and boundary difficulties, marital and personality problems, and traumatic life events such as the death, become obvious. The therapist needs to promote and lead family discussions so a decision can be made to emphasize instrumental or expressive-relational approaches. The use of medication would also be therapeutically debated. The individual taking the medicine would have veto power over any decision regarding medication.

Stage 2: Communication and Boundary Issues

Instrumental Versus Expressive-Relational Methods

An expressive-relational approach could include accentuating the family boundary and power organization, perhaps with drawings or family positioning in the office. In this case, father and son team up against the mother. The "story" and current sense of the marital bond are important. If the therapist can facilitate a three-way conversation that includes empathy, accurate listening, looking, touching, and talking (or if the blocks to appropriate communication can be made clearer), then the family may "spontaneously" work out their relationships and decisions.

In a more instrumental approach, the therapist would direct exercises for improving listening, looking, touching, and talking skills. Discussions would be monitored to have the son confront the mother through the therapist, to avoid excessive unilateral confrontation. This family has several issues: excessive distance (vacations of mother, not listening to each other, no discussion about the family death), excessive boundary violations (excessive anger on the part of the son), false assumptions presented as fact (by the mother), and excessive support and agreement (by the father). Regarding the marriage, the original marriage "unspoken contract" would be compared to the current "contract." In the instrumental approach, the family is changed toward "healthy" communications and "healthy" flexible boundaries. (I use quotation marks for "healthy" since there can be a debate about what is best. My definition of healthy is primarily "flexible.")

The most effective therapy integrates and bridges supportive methods with directive, connection-enhancing confrontations. Most good family therapists simultaneously give support *combined* with direction toward new possibilities and flexibility, even if identified as primarily supportive or primarily directive.

Biological Versus Environmental Causes

From a biological point of view, 6 months after a family death all members could be suffering from a family biochemical posttraumatic depression and hypersensitivity. Antidepressants or anger management medication could potentially reduce the distance between mother and son and enhance communication. Similarly, but in the opposite direction, father and son have an overly close bond, with father being abstractly supportive and validating without really understanding the issues. Certainly, anger reduction would help the marital negotiations.

From an environmental point of view, the communication difficulty could more simply be considered a dialogue "gap" between generations where the parents wish for safety, productivity, and reasonable respect from a teenager, and the teen wishes autonomy and a chance to try out independent thinking. The marital communication problems could be redefined as the mother's promoting more guidance compared to the father's promoting a *laissez-faire* approach. Both approaches would be seen as valid but as creating conflict and canceling each other out. With accurate listening and better contact, a better narrative could facilitate family relationships and decisions.

Stage 3: Personality Issues

Instrumental Versus Expressive-Relational Methods

In the film, the surviving son's style is to hide his pain and suffering. He does, however, act out suicidally and defiantly. The mother is dominated by her own sense of emptiness and perceived lack of nurturing and support. She repeatedly complains. The father is the "good guy" who tries to placate his wife and son, but seems to hide his rage. Certainly under the stress of a recent death, each person would likely accentuate lifelong personality characteristics. One could speculate that the mother may have identified with lifelong passive/victim/repressive elements in her upbringing and now perhaps identifies with these same qualities in the son; she rejects these qualities in the son and distances from him. The father may be expressing the compassionate, caretaking elements from his upbringing; he seems "allergic" to discipline. With the son, the father is overly supportive; with the wife, he is overly hostile. The expressive-relational approach would be to understand how each individual life story informs a current interaction.

Regarding the marital conflict, one family therapist (Resnik, 1992) humorously describes a "Will Rogers marital partner" (friendly, low boundaries, conciliatory) trying to make contact with a "W. C. Fields marital partner" (cynical, high boundaries, critical). If they are in good contact, hopefully each side will be influenced by the other. In the film, the mother is more like W. C. Fields and the father more like Will Rogers.

Instrumental methods to increase personality flexibility include rituals where family members reverse roles. For example, during alternate periods the father could be the disciplinarian while the mother tries on the friendship style. Another basic therapy method is for family members to "redecide" old interpersonal patterns while role playing old interpersonal dynamics (Robert Goulding, 1997). The father could "redecide" to be more critical, and the mother could decide to nurture herself. Whether internally within each individual or externally between family members, differing personality parts can be integrated through dialogues that include debating the "toxic" and "sunny" aspects of each personality characteristic. The ideal would be for each parent to have instrumental and expressive-relational qualities, rather than being split and polarized.

Biological Versus Environmental Causes

The whole family is under stress and depressed after the death of the son. If this stress were reduced by psychopharmacology, each personality style would be less rigid. Considering biological personality spectrums of thinking, mood, violence, and anxiety, the son appears to have ruminative thinking and worrying qualities, the mother appears to be very anxious with a potential for violence and a compulsive need for frequent vacations, and the father seems too calm and suppressed in all areas. Medications could be considered to modulate these temperaments, creating an opportunity for other personality alternatives to be explored.

As an example of environmental etiology, the mother's personality could be understood from a gender and cultural perspective. She had been trained to be subordinate to her family and sacrifice for the deceased son. Her identity was overly wrapped up in her mother role and the dead son's success. She could be seen, now, as "on strike" from her therapeutic, all-protective role. She could be considered the victim of "super-mom" expectations rather than the villain she seems to be. Perhaps therapy would help create a more productive "revolution."

In the personality phase of family therapy, not only are the individual members of the family more fully understood, but also the personality polarities between individuals are explored and reintegrated. The therapist mediates between family factions urging the status quo and factions urging change, and between factions considering psychopharmacology and factions that are not. Therapy can be individual therapy in front of the family (the author's preference) or individual sessions. Knowledge is quickly applied from the individual session back into an interpersonal conversation.

Stage 4: Transitional and Spiritual Issues

Instrumental Versus Expressive-Relational Methods

Expressive-relational therapy would include the retelling of the dramatic, unnatural death of a family member. The therapist would facilitate discussion of the posttraumatic shock and the mourning process. Certainly, the whole family would experience a profound sense of loss that could be helped with open discussion of feelings, remembrances, sadness, survivor's guilt, and a sense of injustice. The spiritual elements of therapy would be crucial.

From an instrumental standpoint, families can be directed to face loss by understanding previous coping styles (mother's activity, son's isolation, and father's charity) and building on the positive aspects of these styles. In addition, mourning rituals (Imber-Black & Roberts, 1992) can be taught, including, for example, daily 15-minute mourning periods with pictures combined with separate 15-minute periods celebrating life.

Biological Versus Environmental Causes

From a biological view, using medications to help with symptoms, family conflicts, and personality rigidities might help the family face a traumatic loss, work together as a unit, and be able to express the profound grief involved. Medications can be used both in a medical model to address genetic and stress-related biological abnormalities and in a humanistic model to facilitate the expression of feelings and needs.

At the environmental end of the spectrum, gender and cultural issues are especially affecting the mother. The cultural guidelines for marital commitment have diminished over the last three decades. A family therapist who tries to preserve marriages and families would have included the family more after the death and paid more attention to the marital conflict. In addition, the surviving son has all the developmental stresses of adolescence such as sexual, body, and career concerns, as well as the prospect of emancipation. The son would certainly need attention to his individual developmental needs as well.

Therapist Issues

In helping the *Ordinary People* family, a therapist would ideally be capable of both compassionate, kind, facilitative work to understand the death and the various levels of family issues, as well as direct experiments to encourage dialogue and healing. Ideally, the therapist would also be open to considering psychopharmacology for both instrumental goals (targeting symptoms or biological conditions) and facilitating the expression of feelings and thoughts.

Supervision might especially help a therapist view the mother sympathetically rather than critically, as would be the usual response. Also, the therapist would need to be clear about her own values regarding the dissolution of marriages, since it appears that the family unit could have been preserved with appropriate therapy. Therapist supervision regarding issues of death, triangulation, divorce, and personality identification with family members would be important.

☐ Overview of Integration Theories

As the interest in integration has increased over the last few years, several integrative points of view have been developed and influenced the integration of the four dimensions. One key influence is the work of Erving and Miriam Polster (1973, 1999). Although the Polsters' dimensional thinking was developed to expand individual gestalt therapy, the power of integrative thinking along a continuum, spectrum, or dimension can be very helpful for connecting the diversified elements of family therapy and pharmacotherapy.

Polster Dimensional Integration

In the prologue to the collection of Erving and Miriam Polster's writings (1999), the Polsters outline their integrative theory of dimensional thinking. In their view, the integrative therapist incorporates "inconvenient dissonances" by alternating her focus between the extremes represented by any two theoretical positions. A dimension is defined as the continuum or spectrum between two opposing positions. The integration is created when the therapist is "informed by dimensional thinking" rather

POLSTER DIMENSIONS

(1) **Here and Now** versus **Full Time and Space**

(2) **Immediate Events of Living** versus **Storyline**

(3) **Parts** versus **Whole**

(4) **Phenomenological, Fluid Experience** versus **Diagnosis and Classification**

(5) **Actual Experience** versus **Meaning**

(6) **Relationship Sensory Contact** versus **Empathy and Merger**

(7) **Awareness** versus **Action**

(8) **Authentic Human Engagement** versus **Technology**

FIGURE 1.3.

than taking a particular stand along that dimension. Several of the gestalt dimensions are especially relevant to work with families (see Figure 1.3). Applying the Polsters' constructs to the stages of family work helps the therapist incorporate seemingly conflicting family therapy points of view in helping families.

The first relevant Polster dimension is a *here and now focus versus a full consideration of time and space*. In stages 1 and 2 of family therapy, the emphasis is on actual phenomena in the present tense. Later stages of therapy regarding personality and spiritual work emphasize the family's past and future as well as its involvement with the outside community. In any session the therapist has a choice: she can follow the family's presentation of events in the present, with historical past tense or future concerns emerging spontaneously, or she can bring the family's attention to historical or future considerations. For psychopharmacology, it is especially important to have a more formal developmental and three-generational history of relevant data before making recommendations about using medication to modify thinking, mood, violence, or anxiety.

A second Polster dimension relevant for family work is the *immediate events of living versus storyline*. Again, the storyline aspect of working with families becomes more important in later phases of family work, but there are tensions in all phases of work between the immediate experience and a historical context. In family therapy, the storyline is especially useful for "reframing" a difficult symptom, person, or interactional pattern in a larger historical context. It is crucial for therapist and family alike to control scapegoating or blaming a particular family member; understanding the storyline is one antidote to such excessive negativity on the part of the family.

A third relevant dimension is *parts versus whole*. Like systems theory, this dimension implies a constant interplay between the whole family and individuals within the family. Early in family work, the family usually presents an individual as having a problem. The therapist, while understanding and valuing that perception, works with the whole family's interactional pattern and outlines the potential phases of later family work that will emphasize the family as a whole and in a community context. The initial phases of therapy are seen as parts leading to a whole. Paradoxically, the flow of therapy with families can also be seen as the opposite, as whole, complex interactional understandings leading to individual parts (see Pinsof, 1995, below).

The concept of parts versus whole is also relevant to the use of psychopharmacology. In the instrumental/medical model, medication treats the target "part" that is malfunctioning, such as a damaged caudate nucleus from streptococcus that leads to obsessive-compulsive disease (see Swedo, Leonard, Mittleman, Allen, Rapoport, Dow, Kanter, Chapman, & Zabriskie, 1997, below). At the other end of the continuum, medication can help the "whole person" be more connected and expressive.

In understanding the therapist's and family's process for integrating foreground and background issues, it is interesting to note that in focal/parts versus global/whole visual perception, functional MRI brain scans have shown (Stiles, 1997) that focal visual perception occurs mainly in the left temporal lobe and that global visual perception occurs mainly in the right temporal lobe. In both individual perceptual development and family functioning, the ideal condition is to have both foreground (focal/parts) and background (global/whole) perceptions integrated. In the integration of the stages of therapy, the therapist and family decide what are the foreground versus background issues. The constant interplay between points along this dimension is optimal in order to integrate immediate and contextual issues.

A fourth important Polster dimension relevant to family work is the continuum of *phenomenological, fluid experience versus diagnosis and classification*. This spectrum is relevant in each phase of family work and in the use of pharmacotherapy. One use of pharmacology is based on biological classifications of genetic or environmental biological dysfunction. Another use of pharmacology is to enhance fluid experience and expression. This two-sided view of psychopharmacology is relevant for each stage of therapy. Polster also stresses the importance of identifying and classifying personality characteristics while encouraging a reintegration of these characteristics to create a feeling of personal "wholeness."

The instrumental model uses diagnosis for research as well as establishing clear goals for change. The fluid, expressive-relational model emphasizes a spontaneous, natural flow of events. Reconciling the polarized extremes of this dimension is also important for integrating the best of competing schools of family therapy and for understanding factions within families that work in a segmented rather than an integrated fashion.

A fifth relevant dimension is *actual experience versus horizontal and vertical meaning*. Although the actual experience is valued, the family is asked to appreciate the meaning of the sequence of events (horizontal meaning) in terms of reinforcing behaviors or in terms of boundary implications. Vertical meaning—the replaying of patterns over time—is especially important in personality work. The search for meaning can be off-putting for the family if the therapist either overly imposes a sequential analysis of current patterning or overly interprets the family as unconsciously reenacting old issues.

A crucial point in the stages of therapy is creating a therapeutic alliance through which both horizontal and vertical meanings can gradually be addressed. In spiritual work, meaning is desired; in scientific work, actual events are emphasized. Again, dimensional concepts open the door for potential integration of two opposite points of view. As an example, patients and families have a wide variety of experiences—from extremely positive to extremely negative—which may come into play while considering or taking medication. The therapist can either take these reactions at face value or look for interpersonal or historical meaning. Integration implies a constant interplay and awareness of both ends of the continuum of experience versus meaning.

The sixth dimension, *relationship sensory contact versus empathy and merger*, describes contact at the boundary where self and other meet, versus empathy and merger, all as parts of a continuum. This relationship dimension is especially relevant in understanding the family boundary and bonding issues of stage 2 work. Families tend to present with overly close, or overly distant, relationship engagement.

Different schools of family therapy emphasize either empathy or accurate communication as the key to stage 2 work or the key to therapist-family interaction and healing. By understanding both the family's and the therapist's strengths and weaknesses in empathy versus accurate sensory contact, again, optimal integration can be achieved.

Medications have historically been emphasized for "reality testing" and "reality contact." A more current view is that the total interpersonal relationship, including empathy, can be enhanced through medication. On the other hand, if the family is enmeshed or overly merged, medication can benefit relationships by increasing boundaries and reducing excessive empathy and merger.

A seventh Polster dimension is *awareness versus action*. The Polsters' "awareness" concept is similar to the nondirective, paradoxical change theories in family therapy. Their "action" concept is similar to the theories that encourage action and direction for corrective possibilities at each stage of family work. Medications have frequently been misused if the therapist is overly preoccupied with action and change. However, medications can encourage awareness without action. Whether it is between complementary family members or between a complementary therapist and family, the ideal integration includes both awareness and action.

Another relevant dimension presented by the Polsters is *authentic, normal, human engagement versus technology*. A basic view of the author is that families can benefit by integration along this continuum, especially if the technology is presented openly, respectfully, and collaboratively. Technology itself ranges from obvious external tools, such as biofeedback or medication, to a more subtle use, such as analysis of transference.

Medication and nonmedication techniques can promote awareness in addition to correcting symptoms or trying to create change. For example, if a therapist working with a depressed family asks each family member to begin several sentences with "I feel sad when . . . " usually the sad affect is accented by including details. Yet this is still a technique, as opposed to a natural, spontaneous conversation about the family's feelings. More stereotypically, techniques or homework are used to create change, hopefully collaboratively with the family. Even nondirective family therapists subtly encourage families to change with questions such as "What gets in the way of this family feeling better?" Obviously, psychopharmacology is an external technology for changing symptoms, boundaries, temperaments, and tolerance for life change or stress. The expanded application of psychopharmacology for family work involves medication to facilitate relationships and the natural interaction between family and therapist.

In summary, in the Polster dimensions, the expressive-relational end of the continuum would include an emphasis on the here and now, immediate events of living and storyline, phenomenological fluid experience, empathy, relationship sensory contact, awareness, and authentic human engagement. The instrumental end of the continuum, using the Polster dimensions, would include a full diagnostic history, a prognosis, diagnosis and classification, vertical and horizontal meaning, action toward change, and the use of technology. The Polsters have a preference for the expressive-relational aspects of therapy, but at the same time seek a flexible, integrative dimensional theory that leaves room for the full range of the instrumental versus expressive-relational considerations.

Although the Polsters' thinking is based on individual therapy, when applied to working with families and psychopharmacology, it has extended the possibilities of family therapy.

Arkowitz's Categories of Therapy Integration

In a book edited by Wachtel and Messer (1997), Hal Arkowitz describes three ways in which therapies can be integrated:

1. by integrating theories
2. by describing common factors
3. through technical eclecticism or combining techniques.

In the first category, theory integration, Arkowitz cites Wachtel's integration of psychodynamic and behavioral theories as being important historically. The work by Pinsof (1995) and Breunlin et al. (1997), discussed below, also attempts to integrate different theoretical models.

In Arkowitz's second category, common factors, he describes Jerome Frank (1963) and Carl Rogers (1961) as two therapists who promoted the universal relationship enhancement common to all therapies. The Polster dimensional thinking approach described above would also be common to all therapies.

In the third category, technical eclecticism, Arkowitz points out that practitioners frequently combine techniques. For example, in sexual therapies like that of Joseph LoPiccolo (LoPiccolo & LoPiccolo, 1978), sexual behavioral methods are combined with psychodynamic techniques and interpersonal communication to improve sexual and relationship functions.

As suggested in Arkowitz's three categories, this book integrates various theories of family therapy and includes a variety of techniques. The concept of dimensional thinking, however, is a unifying element that can help bridge the various theories and techniques.

Metaframeworks

Breunlin, Schwartz, and MacKune-Karrer in their book *Metaframeworks: Transcending the Models of Family Therapy* (1997) have outlined six core metaframeworks, each describing a major school of family therapy (see Figure 1.4). The Breunlin metaframeworks have been placed in the order that follows the stages of therapy. Each stage of therapy is represented by

(1) Sequences	(3) Developmental	(5) Gender
(2) Organizational	(4) Multicultural	(6) Internal Systems

FIGURE 1.4. Metaframeworks (Breunlin et al., 1997).

a major school of family therapy thinking:

- systemic (process)
- structural (form)
- dynamic (historical)
- existential (evolutionary).

In the metaframeworks vocabulary, this staging of therapy would be from the sequences metaframework to the organizational metaframework to the developmental metaframework. The multicultural and gender metaframeworks would apply to all stages, but would be especially discussed with other universal challenges of life in stage 4 (transitions and spirituality). The internal systems metaframework would help organize all the other frameworks; there is some overlap of systems thinking and the dimensional concepts presented. Breunlin invites clinicians and families to use all of the core frameworks outlined.

The *sequences metaframework* describes strategic theory and family therapy. An individual symptom is reinforced or discouraged and develops meaning by the sequence of responses in the family.

The sequences metaframework is crucial to stage 1 family work and is relevant to the flow from stage to stage (Haley, 1973; Watzlawick, Weakland, & Fisch, 1974).

The *organizational metaframework* (leadership, balance, and harmony) is influenced by the structural school of family therapy, with its attention to power arrangements, skews and schisms, and boundaries. Existing family organization can be joined or changed, depending on the therapist. Triangulation, with two people excluding a third or one member of a family protecting two others, would be a central concern of this framework (e.g., Bowen, 1978; Bergman, 1985; Minuchin, 1974).

Stage 2 work, with its emphasis on boundary and communication issues, encompasses many of the same issues described for this metaframework.

The *developmental metaframework* goes beyond simple life-cycle changes for families. It includes cycles from generation to generation, the recognition of blended and stepfamilies having special developmental characteristics, and the interaction between individual development and family development.

The concepts of this developmental framework are especially important in stage 4, life transitions therapy, but also inform the continuum from stage 1–4. Individual development, in an interpersonal context, is discussed as part of stage 3 therapy.

The *multicultural metaframework* examines the importance of cultural influences, patterns of migration, intergenerational practices, and the cultural fit between therapist and family. In addition, it outlines influences of economics, education, religion, gender, and age.

The concepts of this framework inform all the stages of therapy and are crucial for understanding the context of each stage. These concepts are usually more explicitly discussed in stage 4 work regarding universal life stress, transitions, and spirituality.

The *gender metaframework* outlines the impact of feminism on the field of family therapy. This framework addresses the problems of patriarchy and asks, for example, for greater relationship and ecological sensitivity. Women are not assumed to have stereotypic roles such as "homemaker." Instead, a balanced gender view, organizationally, internally, and externally, is promoted for women and men. A gender-aware therapy would amplify awareness of imbalance and encourage less gender-based constraint.

Gender issues inform each of the stages of therapy and are discussed as part of the ongoing process of therapy, such as when addressing marriage inequalities. Also, gender issues are frequently a more specific focus for stage 4.

The *internal systems framework* emphasizes systems theory as applied to families. Although originally designed to describe external systems, the authors (especially Schwartz) describe the internal family of parts and systems thinking as being important clinically. These inner parts are seen as paradoxically both interconnected and autonomous.

The internal systems framework as described for families overlaps in many ways with the gestalt dimensional thinking regarding parts versus whole and with Erv Polster's personality integration work in *A Population of Selves* (1995). The holistic and systems thinking of this framework is included in the continua of foreground versus background, instrumental versus expressive-relational, biological versus environmental, and family self-support versus external support, which are the main themes of this book.

The Pinsof Integrated Family Therapy Model

Pinsof also attempts to integrate the various schools of family therapy in his book *Integrative Problem-Centered Therapy* (1995). Pinsof presents family work as progressing from interpersonal, here-and-now work, to more individual intrapsychic and historical work. His perspective helps the family and therapist consider organizational issues, biological issues, meaning, transgenerational issues, and interpersonal/intrapsychic issues. Like the systems metaframework described above, consideration of multiple aspects of therapeutic work prevents rigidity at any one level and creates a therapeutic harmony, much like integrating parts of a personality creates personality harmony and a potential for relationship harmony.

What will be added to the Pinsof model is the integration of clinical psychopharmacology as well as spiritual issues in family therapy. Also presented is the paradoxical reverse of the Pinsof model, that is, simple problem-solving leading to more complex personality and spiritual considerations.

The Fava Pharmacology/Cognitive-Behavioral Therapy Combination Model

The Italian psychiatrist Giovanni Fava (whose brother Maurizio is in Boston) describes (Fava, Rafanelli, Grandi, Conti, & Bolluardo, 1998) a three-phase model that integrates differing instrumental techniques for depression. The first phase involves antidepressants to relieve severe depressive symptomatology. In his view, a second phase of cognitive behavioral therapy (Beck, Rush, Shaw, & Emery, 1979) can take the place of medication and lead to longer lasting results than medication would. Fava's third phase uses spiritual, cognitive/behavioral methods where patients document positive experiences (relationships, productivity, and feelings of satisfaction) that go beyond a simple absence of depressive symptoms. The cognitive-behavioral component of this positive system is to recognize what thoughts or behaviors take the person out of the state of "well-being." Although Fava integrates environmental and biological concepts, he makes no attempt to integrate instrumental and expressive-relational concepts.

Fava's work parallels one of the goals in this book: to help families first focus on surface problems, but then to also develop the structural, developmental, and spiritual flexibility to enhance the possibility of happiness and well-being. Fava uses primarily instrumental methods of medication plus cognitive-behavioral therapy, while presented here is an integration of both instrumental and expressive-relational methods.

The Serzone/Psychotherapy Combination Study

David Dunner, from the University of Washington in Seattle, has outlined preliminary results from the first clear research that demonstrates the increased benefits of combining psychotherapy and pharmacotherapy compared to using either alone. In a 12-site study for treatment of chronic depression, Serzone (a serotonin-enhancing antidepressant, 600 mg/day) was compared to an eclectic psychotherapy for long-term depression. The psychotherapy emphasized a detailed understanding of real-life interpersonal situations, a dynamic historical perspective regarding depressive attitudes, and cognitive/behavioral methods for reducing depression. Serzone helped 50% of the depressed patients, psychotherapy helped 50%, and the combination helped 85%. Although not family therapy *per se*, the psychotherapy used the interaction of multiple levels as described in this book. The first publication from this $20 million study appeared in the May 2000 issue of *The New England Journal of Medicine* (Keller, McCullough, Klein, Arnow, Dunner, Gelenberg, Markowitz, Nemeroff, Russell, Thase, Trivedi, & Zajecka, 2000). The lead authors were Martin Keller of Brown University and James McCullough, who developed the psychotherapy method.

Breunlin, Pinsof, Fava, and the Serzone study all illustrate efforts to include multiple theories and techniques in clinical practice. Their efforts demonstrate the trend toward combining approaches for helping families. Hopefully, the four-dimensional model presented throughout this book will further the practical clinical application of multiple approaches.

☐ Summary

This chapter has reviewed the need for integration in helping families use the many diversified approaches now available. Four dimensions for bridging integration have been described, using as examples the characters and situation in the film *Ordinary People*. The next chapter emphasizes the appropriate use of pharmacology for each stage of family work and discusses the instrumental versus expressive-relational uses of medication.

An Overview of Psychopharmacology in Conjunction with Family Therapy

☐ A Clinical Example: Harry and Wanda

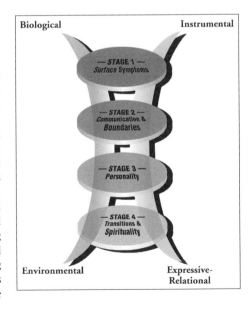

Harry and Wanda, both 70, were a couple who had enjoyed a long-term, successful marriage. After a period of intense, excessive bickering, they contacted me for couples therapy. The husband, Harry, a stoic, successful businessman, had had a series of medical setbacks recently. Prostate surgery had resulted in impotence, he had required shoulder surgery, and his hearing was also significantly reduced from normal. He was also trying to move or sell his business, as well as trying to support the family of one of his two sons.

Harry denied that he was under stress but admitted to having persistent insomnia. Wanda appeared fearful that her husband would either die or be unable to care for her. A history revealed that Wanda had long-standing anxieties and social insecurities that had been covered up over the years by her husband's caretaking behavior toward her.

Stage 1: Therapist Selection and Symptom Definition

Prior to beginning treatment with me, Harry had received treatment from a sleep researcher for his persistent insomnia. The therapy for insomnia had included sleep medications and newer antidepressants. Wanda decided to consult a new therapist and obtained my name from a couple with whom she and her husband were friendly. Wanda's wish to speak to another therapist appeared to reflect her desire for an interpersonal therapy in addition to, or instead of, using medication alone. I suggested scheduling a few sessions to see if we were a good therapeutic match. Medications were not introduced or changed in the initial session, since it was important to honor Wanda's implicit wish for a therapist who would listen, talk, and empathize.

After meeting with the couple and promoting the idea of a truce from fighting, the issue of the medication was introduced. To clarify the dynamics of the symptoms (an expressive-relational approach), I suggested that the husband's insomnia, rather than being a medical condition, was an expression of his stress and anxiety. I also pointed out to Wanda how she had rather passively gone along with her husband's previous medical treatment for insomnia despite her disagreement with it and her growing anxiety that he might die or abandon her emotionally. I suggested that this behavior on her part indicated a tendency to be hesitant, uncomfortable, or self-doubting when it came to expressing her concerns and anxieties directly.

With the reframing of the symptoms, the husband was helped to discontinue all medications (which had included Effexor, Serzone, and Ambien), with the hypothesis that such psychopharmacology treatment was suppressing the expression of his stress and continuing his sleeplessness. After discussion, the wife, previously without medication, was started on low doses of Prozac to help her cope with the changes in her husband and to help her to express her concerns. With this shift, perceptions were rearranged of who was the "patient," unbalancing a previously static system.

The husband began to sleep better, and the wife became more expressive about her concerns and fears. This phase of therapy took 3 months. The information regarding medication was presented openly, and the trial of medication was considered an "experiment." In this way, while medication was initially in the foreground of the therapy, the opportunity for interpersonal reflection and dialogue was also created.

Stage 2: Communication and Boundaries

Both Harry and Wanda were encouraged to have caring time rituals, where they attended to each other rather than his sports or TV or her bridge and lunches with girlfriends. In therapy sessions, Harry would discuss his agenda of five or six areas of stress. Such revelations were new, and Wanda initially expressed frustration instead of compassion, complaining, for example, that when Harry used earphones while watching TV, he cut off contact with her.

With guidance and the help of Prozac, Wanda did express her fears that Harry would become disabled and her feelings of abandonment. Harry initially found these fears to be irrational since he had provided for Wanda, but gradually he began to appreciate Wanda's perception. As Harry had more sleep, he was better able to listen to Wanda. In this stage of therapy, the medication helped Wanda make better contact with Harry because her anxiety and fearfulness diminished. A new level of intimacy began to develop between them.

Stage 3: Personality Issues

As the marital situation improved, Wanda was invited to join, as an individual, a weekly therapy group that I conduct. The Prozac had been helping Wanda with increased communication in her bridge group and with Harry, and Wanda agreed that experience in a social group situation would help her to feel less overly dependent on her husband.

During the next 2 months, however, Wanda began to feel an intense anger toward men in general, the Catholic schools she had gone to, and toward her mother. She expressed these feelings openly in group therapy and reported a new awareness, accompanied by intense anger, of how she had felt dominated and controlled by others in her life. Wanda said that she felt like an overly rigid "Olympic gymnast," where all movements were "robot-like." She felt a new sympathy with women's issues as presented on TV or in group therapy.

Prozac seemed to help this "awareness," but its effect contributed to a therapeutic dilemma, because Wanda suddenly said that she needed a divorce from Harry. Harry, although sleeping better and feeling improved as the real stressors in his life diminished, continued to promote his pretherapy belief that he was strong and the wife weak. Although Wanda felt "ordered around like a dog," she was urged to discuss the raw feelings in group therapy and encouraged to present a more balanced and diplomatic version of her feelings to Harry.

In subsequent conjoint sessions, the husband's "minimizing" and the wife's "maximizing" styles became less polarized over time as each moved more toward a middle ground. The crisis of divorce abated and the couple has stayed together, but the previous definition of Harry as "strong" and Wanda as "weak" has been changed to a more balanced power relationship characterized by more mutual respect and mutual dependency.

Stage 4: Transitions and Spiritual Support

With the experience of discontinuing medications for Harry and starting Prozac for Wanda, the couple began discussing their fears about death, that is, who might die first, the losses associated with impotence, how they would like to divide their estate, and especially how Wanda could cope if Harry died first. They made a decision to stay in their home, even though a move to a simpler condominium had been considered. The symptoms and interpersonal rigidities that had previously prevented an open discussion of this very important dilemma for the couple had been ameliorated and a more open, peer-like relationship had developed, which allowed them to share ideas more freely and make decisions more effectively.

As the couple discussed their real concerns and fought less, the Prozac was discontinued for Wanda. The couple added some meditation and acupuncture with a different therapist. Although Harry was more formally religious than Wanda, both appeared to receive support from knowing that their transitional stresses were universal. The bickering was supplanted by an increased appreciation of the greater issues of enjoying life and intimacy despite aging, disabilities, and disillusions. The group therapy also gave Wanda the sense that she could survive alone, if necessary.

In this clinical example, medication was prescribed and discontinued to help increase expression and communication and to unbalance the perception of who was the patient. In this context, the wife was able to explore her long-term resentments, and eventually the couple could discuss their immediate life transition issues—aging, disability, and approaching death.

The gender split in this couple reflects the instrumental and expressive-relational dichotomy discussed later in this chapter, with the husband more stoic and practical and the wife more reactive and interpersonally experiential. By making each position softer and understandable to the other, the best of both worlds could be partly shared. The end result was a better ability to cope with life's universal issues, which require some practical response as well as a sense of spiritual acceptance. Medication was used with the wife to promote practical strength and useful emotional awareness and containment. Medication was discontinued in the husband when such medication promoted excessive suppression of emotion and affect.

In this therapy, problem-solving with the help of medication was integrated with a dynamic understanding of family structure, personalities, and development. The concept here is not too different from combining behavioral methods for phobias, children's discipline, or sexual disorders, with a more contextual understanding of family or individual dynamics. Frequently, work in the behavioral or deconditioning arenas enhances the contextual awareness and dynamic work, and vice versa (Resnikoff, 1995; Resnikoff & Lapidus, 1990, 1998).

☐ Applying Psychopharmacology in Each Stage of Family Therapy

As has been seen with Harry and Wanda, psychopharmacology can be an asset at each stage of family therapy. However, it will only be an asset if the therapist fully appreciates the stage of therapy that the family is in and what information this tells about them (Solomon, 1977). Without this information, the psychopharmacological aspects of the family therapy may be resisted, rejected, misunderstood, or used in other ways that would prove detrimental to the therapy.

Stage 1: Therapist Selection and Symptom Definition

Therapist Selection

Families choose therapists in a multitude of ways. For instance, if the more instrumental approach dominates the family, they may choose a therapist whom they feel will approach the problem through a pragmatic, problem-solving style. This type of family usually expects medications to be used and might be anxious or confused if the subject of medication is not brought up early. Frequently, such families will bring up the issue of medication themselves if the therapist fails to do so early on. In addition, the leader in an instrumental family may resist therapy altogether so that he or she can remain the "therapist" by default. In this case, one spouse might send the other spouse alone, or with the children, to therapy.

If the expressive-relational view predominates, then getting help from an outside professional may feel relatively comfortable to the family, and seeking support and understanding may seem more crucial than a quick fix. In these families, early introduction of the subject of medication might be off-putting or feel premature. Families such as these see therapy as a process, a gradual unfolding, and feel misunderstood when therapists introduce psychopharmacology early on.

Stereotypically, if an instrumental-style man in the family has selected the therapist, the therapist would be wise to consider that the family as a whole may be characterized by the instrumental style. Conversely, if an expressive-relational type of woman brings the family into therapy, the therapist should bear in mind that the family may lean more toward the expressive-relational style. Exceptions are common, and one goal of stage 1 therapy is to give the therapist the opportunity to determine the predominant style of the family by assessing how therapist selection took place and, thus, measure the family's need for quickly or gradually introducing the issue of medication.

Unfortunately, the environment of managed care, which is so predominant today, favors the instrumental family. Due to the brevity of the therapeutic contract in managed care, the issue of medication is introduced early on, usually in the first session. This is inappropriate for expressive-relational families. It leaves them feeling dissatisfied and may be at the root of the high rate of patient noncompliance with medication, as well as the commonly expressed dissatisfaction with therapy that families voice in the managed care environment.

Symptom Definition

In stage 1, the family's own mechanisms for relieving symptoms are clarified so that the therapist can integrate psychopharmacology appropriately into the family's current patterned responses. For example, instrumental families will lean toward corrective, practical methods for dealing with symptoms. For these families, therapists might introduce behavioral techniques such as direct communication of grievances, "holding" techniques, "good cop/bad cop" parenting strategies, use of the strongest leader of the family as a "cotherapist," reward systems, and so on.

In expressive-relational families, the families are more amenable to the idea that symptoms are a "cry for help" or a metaphor for the family's stress. The family will expect the therapist to clarify the dynamics of the symptoms and provide empathic support so that the family can grow toward greater flexibility. In these families, awareness is promoted through an interpersonal approach (see Zinker, 1994) and a focus on how the family's sequence of events rewards or encourages problem behaviors that are related to anxiety, mood, thinking, or violence. Frequently, symptoms are also maintained to hide marital problems. With appropriate support, expressive-relational families can often reverse the detouring of conflict and can place the issues back into the marital system where they can be worked on more appropriately.

Introducing psychopharmacology during stage 1 with the instrumental family involves pairing psychopharmacological treatments with the behavioral techniques discussed above. Instrumental families are likely to appreciate and value the clear-cut "change" possibilities of medication, as well as cognitive/behavioral methods (see Resnikoff, Stein, & Diller, 2000). With these families, medication is presented as having individual biological consequences. Ritalin is introduced as the drug used for attention deficit disorder (ADHD); Risperdal, Zyprexa, or Seroquel for delusions, hallucinations, and anhedonia; Prozac and other serotonin-enhancing drugs (SSRIs) for depression, social phobia, obsessive-compulsive disorder, panic disorder, and so on (Stahl, 2000). Of course, the behavioral techniques are also prescribed. The similarity in these methods is that some expert influence is added to the family system externally, and the family follows the advice and prescriptions of the therapist.

In expressive-relational families, the therapist clarifies and reflects the system as it exists, so that the family gains greater self-awareness and can make changes. The therapist does not influence the system from the outside, for the most part. With these families, medication that is introduced during stage 1 must be presented as an option that can help the family make better use of the therapy. Although the same medications are used as mentioned above, they are presented as providing underlying support that will help the family better tolerate the stress of therapy, rather than as "silver bullets" targeting certain symptom constellations. The use of medication to support therapy is not just another "spin" or manipulation. Instead, the expressive-relational use of medication is openly discussed as part of a continuum regarding how medications can be incorporated.

The therapeutic challenge in stage 1 is to honor both the instrumental and expressive constructs. In practice, the family's instrumental versus expressive spectrum can be explored by asking the family to imagine what the ideal magic pill would bring about, and clarifying both the individual biological consequences and the expressive-relational consequences of the ideal medication. Through dialogues, the family can begin to integrate any disparate views regarding the "change"/instrumental versus the "no change"/expressive-relational points of view. This exploratory initial method is particularly useful for the majority of cases in which the presenting symptom is not life-threatening and does not require immediate attention.

Stage 2: Communication and Boundaries

In stage 2 the therapist must determine the family's beliefs about the importance of interpersonal contact and how it is established, maintained, and intensified. The expressive-relational model has many rich, long-standing ideas and methods for promoting flexible, appropriate boundaries and connections within the family. Basic ideas such as accurate empathy, active listening, and validation have been emphasized by feminist writers who point out that women, especially, often become angry, depressed, or otherwise symptomatic without these basic human needs being met. Oppressed groups, in general, have been denied a voice to express their concerns.

Gestalt therapy has emphasized developing and practicing "contact functions," essentially using the five senses augmented by verbal exchange (Polster, 1987b). Sometimes heightening the awareness of what is lacking in interpersonal contact can help improve the connection. The best marriages seem to start out with a physical attraction reinforced by matching and bonding along intellectual, cultural, recreational, and professional dimensions. Therapy can help couples toward bonding and toward mutual tolerance in areas where bonding is lacking.

Psychopharmacology has not usually been considered as a means of promoting or facilitating an interpersonal connection. In fact, one criticism of pharmacology in therapy is that real contact, hypnosis, or bonding does not occur between patient and therapist if the patient is drugged. This point of view maintains that the appropriate use of medication is to correct a localized, biochemical malfunctioning in the brain. As mentioned in the Preface, behavior therapy coordinates well with this view of medication, since for many diagnoses (for example, obsessive compulsive disorder (OCD)), both behavioral techniques and pharmacological treatments can correct underlying abnormalities in the brain as recorded in PET scans (J. Schwartz, 1995). For instrumental families, medication is about changing the brain, not about facilitating interpersonal connections; instrumental families would appreciate both the behavioral and medication modalities as having a clear effect.

On the other hand, it is possible that an amphetamine can help one person focus or pay attention more fully to another. Certainly, if a person is preoccupied by depressive thoughts, pain, or fears, controlling these with medication will free the patient to consider interpersonal input and will better allow them to experience interpersonal support and encouragement. Clearly, for manic illness or schizophrenia (Lithium or Depakote for mania; and Zyprexa, Risperdal, Seroquel, or Clozaril for schizophrenia), medications can control the delusions and distortions of reality that make interpersonal contact nearly impossible. Similarly, with OCD, Zoloft or Luvox can help control obsessions and compulsions so that interpersonal contact and intimacies can become possible. For expressive-relational families, therefore, medication is seen as a means of enhancing interpersonal contact. Again, if the therapist can join the family at the expressive-relational end of the continuum, and medication is considered from a humanistic, communication-enhancing point of view, it is more likely that medication will be used.

The therapeutic challenge of this stage of therapy is to have the family engage both views of medication simultaneously and debate the pros and cons of each view. The therapist can help the family in a collaborative way to consider the costs and benefits of medication in terms of enhanced contact and communication, as well as treatment for biochemical conditions. The collaborative approach and focus on enhanced contact are more comfortable for expressive-relational families; the discussion of the biochemical treatment is not. Shifting away from the medical model and the hierarchical treatment relationship is more uncomfortable for instrumental families; the discussion of ameliorating underlying brain malfunctioning is not. Only by developing the dialogue about these polar views can both types of families appreciate all of the issues involved in medication. Then they can make a fully informed choice that will help avoid acting out around the medications and lessen patient noncompliance.

Stage 3: Personality Issues

If psychopharmacological and family therapy intervention have been introduced appropriately in stages 1 and 2, then changes are already being felt within the family system. In stage 3, the therapist must monitor the interpersonal personality changes within the family as one person receives medication. In some families, personality corrections will be welcome and supported. In other families where projective processes dominate, personality corrections will be sabotaged, and any medication improvements will be overwhelmed by the underlying pressure to preserve long-standing pathological patterns (Minuchin, Rosman, & Baker, 1978). Some families simply do not accept healthy change, needing to have a scapegoat or someone who is designated symbolically to represent other family members' issues.

Since personalities in families are often polarized or opposite, a shift in one member usually creates a systems shift, either in a healthy accommodating way or in a backlash way. For example, if a woman becomes more clear and assertive on Prozac, her husband has a choice of enjoying the better, healthier dialogue or, conversely, escalating his power to counteract what he perceives as a threat (Michael Miller, 1995).

Since the goal of psychopharmacological intervention in stage 3 is to ultimately achieve flexible, effective communication among family members without excessive personality distortion, the therapist will want to closely monitor the family's response to the changes brought about by the medications. When medications are working positively, personality manifestations will move more toward a middle ground (Siever & Davis, 1991). Larry Siever suggests the possibility of using low doses of drugs on a longer-term basis to stabilize temperament, rather than treating overt symptomatology with higher doses of drugs. If the temperamental style of a family member is less rigid, better interpersonal listening and dialogue will be enhanced. (Chapter 5 includes a further discussion of psychopharmacology, temperament, and personality interpersonal therapy.)

Stage 4: Transitions and Spiritual Support

Transitions

Some families and individuals cope better with transitions, stress, and changes, than do others. Standard therapies help to promote awareness of external pressures and help develop ego skills to cope. Finding historical, positive coping stories can be especially helpful in the family.

Sometimes situations overwhelm an individual's ability to cope. For example, one psychiatrist described helping the Armenian earthquake victims of 1988. In this situation, medication with Prozac and the strongly held religious beliefs of the populace seemed much more helpful than therapy. Therefore, the challenge for the therapist must be to determine when stressors are beyond the human's threshold for pain—whether physical or emotional—and medication is needed (see Shuchter, 1986). This determination can best come about through a dialogue within the family.

Should Xanax be offered for the stress of a wedding or funeral? Should sleep medications such as Ambien or Sonata be offered, or should the person stay up and become aware of the life issues interrupting sleep? Certainly, there is no one correct view.

The therapist's job at this stage of therapy is to help mediate an informed therapeutic debate within the family system about the use of psychopharmacology for the stress of life transitions. By working collaboratively with the family, the therapist can help instrumental families discover hidden resources and strengths within themselves as individuals and within the family as a whole that might help them cope with developmental transitions, psychological stress, or environmental change. Similarly, the therapist can help expressive-relational families consider the possibility that relief from suffering can be avoided with minor medical risk, and that such reduction of unnecessary suffering may be desirable.

Spiritual Support

Many individuals and families crave spiritual support and the sense of feeling part of a larger, meaningful process. Paul Fleischman (1990) has described the overlap of spiritual and clinical work. His thinking is discussed in detail as part of Chapter 6. Families provide a mini spiritual arena where security, a sense of continuity, concerned interest, and faith all have a part. Interestingly, drugs or alcohol have been a part of spiritual rituals for centuries, helping people access feelings of hope and faith without being unduly blocked by distracting cognitions. Although spiritual concerns provide a contextual backdrop for therapy, they are often initially overshadowed by symptoms. In the later phases of therapy, however, spiritual issues are more in the foreground.

In this last stage of therapy, the therapist must create an integration between the mechanistic, scientific, linear beliefs about medication characteristic of the instrumental family and the more holistic, intuitive, and circular beliefs about medication characteristic of the expressive-relational family. Without this integration, the instrumental family remains blocked to deeper spiritual issues, thinking of medication only as a silver bullet that kills the undesirable symptom. This type of family needs to engage the holistic model of how the medication relates to all of the systems in the body, and how the medicated family member relates to the larger family system.

Similarly, without a therapeutic dialogue, the expressive-relational family may continue to think of medication as mysterious and may remain resistant to accepting underlying biochemical and physiological differences among family members that influence behavior. Although expressive-relational families are more amenable to considering deeper, spiritual issues, they often minimize the role that medication plays in actually altering biochemistry; thus, they may not take medication regularly, stop taking medication too soon, or take it improperly.

☐ Previous Approaches

As has been seen, psychopharmacology can be used at different stages of family therapy to promote awareness, understanding, and communication, similar to the expressive-relational schools of family therapy. At the same time, psychopharmacology can be used to promote practical problem-solving, reduce target symptoms, and improve personality functioning, similar to the instrumental schools of family therapy.

Similarly, some books on psychopharmacology propose medications as part of a symptom-reduction strategy in helping families, and other books propose medications as part of a communication-enhancing process that promotes healing more indirectly. An example of the instrumental, medical-model use of psychopharmacology is a book by David Miklowitz and Michael Goldstein, *Bipolar Disorder* (1997), in which a family-focused treatment approach for bipolar disorder is developed. In this book, bipolar disorder is described as a clear medical disorder requiring special control and medication. Family support systems are seen as potentially part of the problem or part of the solution.

A contrasting example of the communication-enhancing or "narrative" use (see White & Epston, 1990) of psychopharmacology is outlined by James Griffith in his book *The Body Speaks* (Griffith & Griffith, 1994). His approach encourages open discussion with the help of medication to facilitate healing in families with psychosomatic illness. Griffith points out that medications have frequently been misused for controlling or suppressing patients' complaints rather than for facilitating a deeper understanding of personality issues and underlying vulnerabilities. Such misuse can create a destructive hierarchical relationship between therapist and patient or family, with the therapist having excessive power. Griffith instead promotes psychopharmacology to facilitate the "narrative" of the family; he

Psychopharmacology in Conjunction with "INSTRUMENTAL" and "EXPRESSIVE-RELATIONAL" Family Therapy Constructs

STAGE OF THERAPY	"INSTRUMENTAL" (practical, directive, strategic, problem-focused, cognitive/behavioral)	"EXPRESSIVE-RELATIONAL" (awareness, clarification, nondirective, narrative, self-psychology, gestalt)
Surface Symptoms Who should I seek therapy with?	**Who?** • Pharmacologist, internist, psychiatrist • Behaviorist, strategic therapist, parenting advisor • Managed care short term problem-solving • Addiction control specialist • Hospital control	**Who?** • Interpersonal healing therapist • Religious counseling • Gender/cultural awareness group • Communal experiences
How can family suffering be reduced?	**What?** • Medication for disorders of thinking, mood, violence, anxiety • Behavioral/cognitive control • Change behavioral sequence around symptom	**What?** • Medication for symptom clarification • Awareness of symptom as metaphor • Awareness of family contextual influence on symptom • Awareness of gender/ cultural context of symptom • Story of symptom
Communication and Boundary issues How can communication and flexible boundaries be enhanced?	• Medication to reduce distractions from thinking, mood, violence, anxiety disorders • Medication to lower or raise boundaries • Reduce distractions with artificial structure • Change leadership and family structure to create balance	• Medication that enhances narratives and dialogues. • Awareness of communication blocks • Awareness of rigidities of closeness/distance • Enhancing narratives • Awareness of gender/cultural influences on family communication/structure
Personality issues What are the personality polarities in the family and how is personality flexibility enhanced?	• Medication to modify temperaments including thinking, mood, violence, anxiety • Exercises to promote flexible personalities • Exercises to rewrite old scripts	• Medication that helps discussion of issues and personality differences • Awareness and clarification of styles including 3-generational patterns and projections • Polarity dialogues • Awareness of gender/cultural influences on personality
Transitional and spiritual issues What are the genetic, environmental and transitional limitations the family must cope with? What spiritual coping tools can be included?	• Medication to reduce life stress • Medication to support previous coping style • Actively label and support family or individual's successful coping style • Directed areas of therapeutic spiritual concern: faith, acknowledgment, lawful order, life meaning • Medication to promote spiritual, transpersonal experiences	• Medication to facilitate awareness of universal transitional and spiritual issues. • Gently accentuate life transition impasse • Empathic support and comfort during universal transitions • Awareness of gender/cultural influences on transitions and spiritual values • Unspecified spiritual aspects of therapy: safety sense of universality, meaning, order

FIGURE 2.1.

creates an emphasis on "vulnerabilities" rather than "diseases." Griffith also emphasizes the therapist working in collaboration with the family rather than as an "expert" or imposing her own will. In short, Griffith emphasizes the empowering aspects of medication.

Also supporting the use of medication for enhanced social behavior, Owen Wolkowitz (Knutson, Wolkowitz, Cole, Chan, Moore, Johnson, Terpstra, Turner, & Reus, 1998) has described the use of serotonin enhancing agents (Paxil) in increasing the sense of well-being, friendliness, and a positive outlook in "normal" volunteers. His research subjects had no psychiatric diagnosis or apparent emotional problems. Wolkowitz supports the notion that medication can work by enhancing personality functioning rather than by correcting diseases or pathology.

In a broader context, for at least the past 30 years, there has been an interest, but difficulty, in integrating the biological and psychosocial fields (Gabbard, 1996). Biological symptom-focused methods have generally been separated from methods emphasizing family dynamics or societal forces. There has been some integration in the field of psychosomatic medicine. The Medical Family Therapy Model (McDaniel, Hepworth, & Doherty, 1995) has been especially effective in expanding the bio-psycho-social concepts of George Engel (1977), which bridge medical scientific thinking with psychosocial processes (see Rolland, 1994).

To expand Griffith's complaints about the change-oriented, practical problem-solving model, objections to psychopharmacology have included misuse of medication in all of the following ways:

- to excessively suppress symptoms or complaints
- to avoid psychological or systems issues
- to excessively shame the family with the concept of "disease"
- to use the concept of a medication crutch in a demeaning way
- to excessively blame or label one member of a family as the cause of family problems
- to gratify grandiose healing impulses of the physician
- to exploitatively promote research or profit
- to mistakenly either change or support the family structure when the opposite is clinically indicated.

Thomas Szasz (1988) has also been an outspoken critic of psychopharmacology as frequently used for control and domination, even if promoted in a paternal, caretaking manner.

Awareness, expressive-relational schools of family therapy help clarify family symptoms, organizational patterns, and interpersonal dynamics. Effective expression and listening are seen as crucial healing factors. Regarding awareness and understanding approaches to family therapy, Jean Miller (1991; Miller & Stiver, 1997) points out that "feminine" expertise in connectability, empathy, and support has been overlooked in our culture in favor of more "masculine" competitive, hierarchical, problem-solving models that emphasize autonomy and independence. She points out that pharmacology is frequently overused for less powerful groups, such as women.

Similarly, Miriam Polster (1992) has described feminine (as opposed to masculine) heroism as the ability to mediate and form relationships in contrast to more goal-directed traditional heroism. Authors such as these have helped us to become aware of the differences between "feminine" expressive (or relational) abilities and "masculine" instrumental abilities.

Being more aware of this instrumental versus expressive-relational continuum, it becomes possible for the contemporary practitioner who uses psychopharmacology to use a therapeutic model that integrates the characteristics of both the instrumental and the expressive-relational approaches. This integration would include a medical, biological model focusing on brain etiologies for mental illness, as well as a psychosocial model focusing on relationships, connections, and empathy as healing forces.

In clinical practice with families, as described above, the therapist can mediate discussions between instrumental and expressive-relational family members. Michael Fox (1993) has presented a somewhat similar model for the initial phase of family therapy to help the psychopharmacologist or family therapist be part of the healing process instead of simply a technician. His model involves the therapist's mediating between the medication decision-maker (DM) in the family and the decision-implementer (DI) in the family. The DM has leadership qualities at the instrumental end of the continuum. The DI is at the expressive-relational end of the spectrum. In this mediation, the therapist provides information but minimizes her own decision-making role; the therapist helps the family decide if, when, and how to use psychopharmacology.

In addition, the therapist must be aware of her own biases towards drugs. The therapist needs self-awareness regarding whether she might be duplicating (or countering) patterns in the family that also exist in the therapist's family of origin. For example, the most common problem is to overuse medication, either out of a feeling of powerlessness or out of a feeling of omnipotence. If the behavior of the therapist includes an open, nondefensive discussion of these medication issues, then the chances for a humanistic, effective therapy are increased.

Although some psychoanalysts such as Robert Michels (1996, 1997) and others recommend that the therapist who does problem-solving work (or medications) not be the same person who does interpersonal transference work; the author believes the opposite. In the case of Harry and Wanda, family therapy was primarily problem-focused at all stages of therapy, and because transference distortions were quickly corrected rather than developed, there was no contradiction.

When awareness is the primary emphasis (awareness of sensations, interpersonal dynamics, or structure), its purpose is to inform pragmatic changes or decisions. When simple behavioral, practical, or pharmacological approaches solve the problem, then the contextual phases of the therapy can be minimal. In contrast, if the contextual issues reflect long-term engrained patterning, then those phases become more important. Just as with parenting, the therapist's role is flexible, with a range from problem-solving techniques on the one hand, to a philosophy regarding life and death on the other, depending upon the need.

Psychopharmacology must be used differently at each stage in the treatment of a family, although the overriding goal in the use of psychopharmacology remains that of integrating the instrumental and expressive-relational approaches. Each stage of therapy should involve the family in a discussion of what emphasis is needed in either the practical or the awareness aspects of the therapy. Information regarding medication should be presented for consideration, with the therapist having a solid handle on how best to introduce medications in each stage of therapy. The seeming contradiction of offering a practical instrument to enhance expressive-relational interpersonal communication should be addressed openly.

The current concerns regarding the integration of pharmacology on the one hand, and family therapies that emphasize interpersonal awareness and understanding on the other, parallels the long-standing polarity within the larger field of family therapy between strategic/structural (instrumental) methods and psychoanalytic/object relations (expressive-relational) methods. Even as early as the 1960's, therapists were being dichotomized as primarily directors or reactors.

The ideal, however, is an active dialogue between problem-solving and interpersonal awareness constructs. Problem-solving would be emphasized in earlier phases of therapy, but the entire therapy would be seen as helping the family through a life transition.

In summary, family therapy can bridge both pharmacological treatments and basic family therapy principles. This sort of combined approach is more effective than using either approach alone. Because the interpersonal and pharmacology viewpoints are still quite divergent, a sense of integration is needed. To the extent that psychopharmacology can promote awareness and better interpersonal contact, and to the extent that awareness can lead to problem-solving, then the instrumental versus expressive-relational polarities can be bridged.

In the four chapters that follow, each stage of therapy will include a further discussion of psychopharmacology in conjunction with other family therapy approaches.

3
CHAPTER

Stage 1 Therapy: What are the Surface Problems of the Family?

The next four chapters present the staging continuum (surface, communication, personality, and transitions) as four distinct stages of family therapy for clinical and teaching purposes. In any given session, the four staging issues can all be present and overlap. Even in any 5-minute segment, foreground and background issues can both be appreciated. Each chapter, however, highlights the main focus of a particular stage. The dimension of staging helps both the therapist and the family address issues in sequence without being overwhelmed; in addition, the staging dimension reminds the

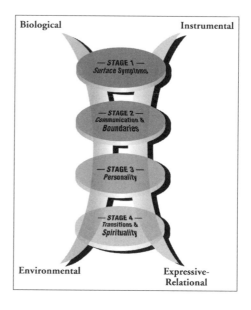

family that there is not just one reductionistic way to consider problems. Having diversified possibilities offers flexibility for helping and change.

Each stage is negotiated with the family. As with other dimensional dialogues, frequently one family member wants to consolidate gains and stop therapy, and another family member wants to continue to consider more complex contextual, background issues. The therapist mediates this discussion, but also may give her own opinion when appropriate.

"What is, is."

This humorous comment by Erv Polster summarizes the philosophy that both therapist and family can accept the problem as the problem, rather than seeing communication/organizational difficulties, personalities, or life transitions as the "real" problem. By addressing surface problems first, the family feels listened to and validated by the therapist for how the family perceives their difficulties.

This chapter provides a number of clinical examples to illustrate instrumental approaches versus expressive-relational approaches to surface issues. It also illustrates the biological versus environmental dimension, which is crucial in considering psychopharmacology. The surface problems are presented to the family as part of a multistaged model of family work that will integrate the dimension of foreground surface issues with background contextual issues.

The family usually presents with an acknowledged surface problem that requires intervention. This call for help is frequently in the form of a child or teenager having some symptomatic difficulty. Depending on the predominant symptom in the family and the bias of the therapist, the therapist will either lean toward a diagnosis of biological and temperamental factors or will lean toward understanding symptoms through interpersonal system dynamics. In the biological versus environmental dimension, primarily biological problems include surface symptoms of illnesses and medical conditions that are seen to be primarily genetic and biological. These include bipolar illness, severe biological depression, attention deficit disorder with hyperactivity, certain obsessive-compulsive states and panic disorders, and hereditary schizophrenic conditions characterized by paranoia, delusions, hallucinations, and a bland expression. At the environmental end of the continuum, surface problems would be seen as primarily the result of the family dynamics, situational stressors, and posttraumatic reactions (although these can also have a biological component), interpersonal patterns over three generations, and gender and cultural influences.

Also depending on the family, the therapist will be inclined either to actively help the family try to correct or change the presenting symptom or, alternatively, to help the family clarify or become more aware of the presenting symptom and sequence of events around that symptom. That is, the therapist will be operating along an instrumental versus expressive-relational continuum. Other terminology for the instrumental mode includes change-oriented, directive, cognitive/behavioral, and psychopharmacological methods for symptom control. The expressive-relational mode includes nondirective, clarifying, awareness-enhancing and psychopharmacological methods designed to help the expression of the presenting problem rather than to control a target symptom.

The therapist becomes an artist when she can help families work flexibly along both these dimensions while considering presenting problems.

☐ Jack's Family

This first clinical example illustrates a family where the therapist perceives a biological problem (bipolar illness), but the family is dichotomized with the mother urging a nonbiological, spiritual approach (expressive-relational) and the father urging a problem-solving practical approach (instrumental) to their son's symptoms. The therapeutic challenge is how to mediate both considerations in working with the immediate surface problem of Jack's delusions and his dropping out of college.

> Jack was a college student who presented with two main delusions. The first delusion was that he was the best guitar player in the world, or at least one of the best, and that the Ziggy Marley group and the Marley followers

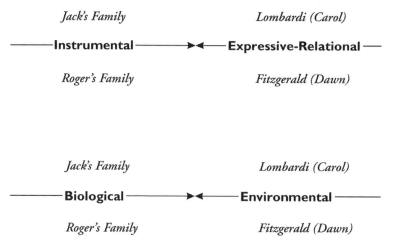

FIGURE 3.1. In the clinical examples, the families (and therapist) in stage 1 therapy (surface symptoms) are helped to bridge instrumental versus expressive-relational methods and biological versus environmental causes. Integration comes about by considering the entire dimension, even though one point of view along the dimension may be more apparent.

were trying to kill him in order to prevent any competition. In a different arena, Jack saw himself as one of the best surfers in the world and, again, he believed there was a conspiracy to hurt him or eliminate him in order to minimize competition. These delusions started after Jack was rejected as a guitar player in a rock and roll band at his college.

In a meeting with the family, the parents had very different approaches to Jack's problem and how to address it. The mother came from a spiritual orientation including visits to spiritual guides. She brought Jack to visit these gurus and used an intuitive, somewhat abstract, belief system in addressing problems. She was initially concerned after one psychiatrist had said that her son was schizophrenic; she was hoping to avoid medications and promote a loving atmosphere away from college. The son was closer to the mother and she had the initial response to his symptoms.

The father, a businessman, had a much more practical approach and disagreed with the mother. He wanted clear steps and medication to help control the symptomatology and felt that the son needed to be more disciplined in his life and studies. With this family, several sessions were held conjointly to allow the family to understand their own sequence of assumptions and to demonstrate and clarify the family's internal struggle in attempting to help Jack.

After the first session with the family, I came to the initial tentative conclusion that, on a biological level, Jack was suffering from a bipolar illness with delusions characterized by grandiosity. This diagnosis, rather than schizophrenia, was also supported by the historical information that Jack had been one of the most popular boys in his high school and had had a number of girlfriends. This background description helped confirm the bipolar diagnosis as opposed to the more typical schizoid history of schizophrenic paranoid delusions. There had been a history of some emotional instability on the mother's side, and the mother herself described some excessive anxiety and sensitivity. From an interpersonal standpoint, it seemed that Jack was in a family dynamic sequence around the surface symptoms, where the mother would be protective and supportive without criticism or confrontation. This stance would be followed by the father's more critical, practical interventions. The family parenting system as a result had two opposite problem-solving styles that interfered with each other and were dysfunctional for Jack's development and treatment, unless coordinated.

Using an expressive-relational approach, I was open and collaborative regarding therapeutic deliberations. I shared with the family the probable biological aspects of the presenting problem as well as the barrier to providing a healing structure for Jack that the parents were creating through their conflicting parenting styles. After discussions with the parents, I expressed my support for the mother's spiritual belief system, but suggested that the father's approach may be more important initially to help control the presenting symptoms and, if possible, have Jack return to college. The mother was also reassured that the medication would help Jack to express his fears and anxieties in therapy.

After an initial drug regimen of Mellaril, an older antipsychotic used briefly for behavioral control but avoided for long-term use because of muscular side effects, Risperdal was added gradually (There has also been a recent drug alert regarding cardiac side effects for Mellaril.). After some stabilization, Depakote was added to further control the manic-depressive symptomatology. After medications, Jack was able to describe more expressively how he felt scrutinized in a movie line or with college roommates as his delusions were first beginning. Within 2 weeks, Jack's delusional symptoms were markedly improved revealing his more basic personality, which included communicating in a jovial way without much specific content but with much personalized jargon such as joking about being "rustifarian." Jack also had a tendency to be irresponsible regarding time, commitments, and concern for other people before and after the development of his delusions.

At this point in stage 1 of the therapy, both parents were urged to alternate their approaches to help Jack feel both emotional support from the mother and practical guidance from the father (rather than cancelling each other out).

In the 1970's, a strategic view of symptom-control developed, through which the family might be maneuvered to change their patterned sequences around the presenting problem. At that time, hypnotic directive techniques were also used to direct the patient and the family away from the symptomatology. Paradoxically, to prove that change is possible, directives were also used to temporarily make symptoms worse. In the 1980's, however, there was a backlash against these more controlling, manipulative methods to a more naturalistic, conversational, contextual understanding of symptoms. Object relations therapists David and Jill Scharff (1987, 1991) have even argued that dealing with surface symptomatology is simply a band-aid that results in recurrence of symptoms unless core issues and core patterning rigidities are addressed.

A basic idea of the author's approach is to use here-and-now phenomenology initially to clarify the symptom and the sequence of events around the symptom. The therapist in stage 1 also gains an immediate sense of the family's communication, personality dynamics, and history that might support the symptom and be addressed more fully in later stages of family therapy. The hope is that by creating some simple improvement and a therapeutic alliance in the surface suffering of the family, the family will become interested in the ongoing process of therapy and will eventually appreciate, if needed, a more complex understanding of the contextual background issues. In addition, the family is helped to actually address the problem and correct it to a certain extent, and sometimes even to resolve the surface problem completely. Any techniques or manipulations are discussed openly with the family and introduced as "experiments."

The therapy for Jack's family tended toward supporting the instrumental, directive change end of the continuum by using medication to control target symptoms of delusions and anxiety. This instrumental stance facilitated the family's understanding of their system dynamics, where the two parents worked against each other, and also facilitated Jack's expression of his suffering. The emphasis was on biological factors, with the bipolar diagnosis implying a potential chronic illness, of which this was a first episode. This biological condition, however, was put in the environmental context of the family dynamics and the stress of Jack's leaving home and going to college. It was hoped that the family would consider ongoing therapy to address the conflicted communication patterns and personality polarities in the family. In addition, the goal was that the family could later address the emancipation issues and the extent to which Jack would be able to tolerate returning to college. David Moltz (1993) has similarly noted the need to include biological individual concerns together with family and social modalities of treatment in helping bipolar patients.

The intent here is to emphasize the first phase of therapy, but this family did move on to later stages. There was subsequent treatment for the sister's attention deficit disorder and depression, as well as marital therapy for the parents' marital issues that had been exposed. In addition, the family has struggled to provide enough support to have the patient return to college. Jack is due to graduate this coming year. Jack currently uses Depakote and attends occasional family therapy sessions. Jack's treatment is an example of a family that was able to integrate addressing surface problems in family work with later stages of family therapy.

☐ Roger's Family

In this next clinical example, a child's dramatic surface behavior is clearly self-destructive and, similarly to the last example, may have a bipolar temperament biological component. The family is very willing to consider an instrumental, biological approach to prevent extreme danger and to create behavioral control. Although there is some controversy between the wife, who is a "maximizer," and the husband, who is a "minimizer," once the child's behavior is controlled, the therapist can more leisurely consider parental conflicts, general control issues in the family, and any transitional issues of an 8-year-old becoming more self-sufficient.

Preventing self-destruction and dangerous out-of-control behaviors becomes a first step to more careful consideration of environmental systems and personality conflicts. The therapeutic alliance has begun. A therapist who focuses only on systemic patterns might say that symptom-focused therapy is reinforcing the scapegoating of the identified patient, who is actually a reflection of a systemic problem. The author believes such systemic concerns become foreground only after the child's safety is assured.

In short, this next clinical example is at the instrumental end of the instrumental versus expressive-relational dimension and is at the biological end of the biological versus environmental dimension. Both dimensions are related to surface issues, although the therapist begins to understand contextual organizational, personality, and transitional issues in the family. Roger's family also illustrates the newer uses of psychopharmacology with children, in a family context.

> An 8-year-old boy, Roger, jumped out of the car and, on another occasion, threatened to kill himself with a knife shortly after the parents had left on vacation. In this family, the father, an accountant, seemed to have an even, extremely controlled temperament, opposite to Roger's. The mother was much closer to Roger and described parental conflicts in handling the situation with the father the "minimizer" and the mother the "maximizer." There was a relative on the father's side with bulimia and another relative with a bipolar disorder.
>
> In a family interview, Roger demonstrated a mixture of surface symptoms. He was obviously anxious and described being very afraid when his parents left home. In addition, he had a flamboyant, talkative style and was extremely engaging, reminiscent of a bipolar temperament. The family reported encopresis (inability to control bowel movements) and periods where Roger seemed to be out of touch with reality, when he would become violent or have screaming temper tantrums.
>
> After consideration of the presenting details of this case and the three-generational history of control/impulse issues, Roger was initially started on Paxil in low doses for anxiety/depression control, and low doses of Depakote to address the bipolar temperament and possible conduct problems related to mania. Although the patient responded somewhat to the two medications, a major tranquilizer, Risperdal, was also added in low doses. The combination of the three drugs created a marked improvement in behavior control after 2 weeks. It should be noted that the use of antidepressants such as Paxil in bipolar conditions has the risk of bringing on a manic episode and has to be monitored carefully.
>
> Hospitalization was avoided, and the suicide potential was reduced. Psychological testing revealed borderline personality characteristics including extreme anxiety, anger, and temporary lapses of reality. In this particular case, a different therapist was treating the family while I was the pharmacology family consultant.

It is important to discuss Roger's family because of the new thinking regarding children's conduct disorders and psychopharmocology. Although conduct disorders have been associated with attention deficit disorder, personality disorders, depression, and other kinds of emotional regulatory problems, Joseph Biederman (Biederman et al., 1999) and his group at Harvard have been especially influential in promoting the concept that a large percentage of children's conduct disorders may actually represent the child's early developmental version of a bipolar manic disturbance. The treatment for such conduct disturbances includes Lithium or Depakote, especially, to address bipolar illness, but major tranquilizers such as Risperdal and Zyprexa have also been used for bipolar illness and conduct disturbance.

Demitri and Janis Papolos, in their book *The Bipolar Child* (1999), have emphasized that ADD, separation panic, OCD, and borderline personality disorder can be reflections of the bipolar spectrum rather than separate diagnoses. These authors believe that the stimulants or antidepressants/antianxiety agents that can assist in managing ADD, panic, OCD, or borderline personalities eventually worsen the rapid cycling of the childhood bipolar condition. The Papoloses suggest either not using stimulants or antidepressants if a bipolar condition is suspected, or at least "protecting" such treatments with "mood stabilizers" such as Lithium or Depakote.

Frequently, the clinician is in a dilemma when there is, for example, a combination of depression or OCD as well as bipolar hypersensitivity. This dilemma is discussed with the treatment family and the author's preference is to use antidepressants very cautiously, protected with "mood stabilizers", in such situations. Currently, Roger is doing well while taking Lithium, Neurontin, and Risperdal. Paxil, a potentially overstimulating antidepression/anxiety medication, has been discontinued.

In Roger's clinical situation, there appeared to be a combination of biological and environmental factors. If the family were more attentive to the separation sensitivity and control issues of the youngster, and if they could help with emotional and physiological regularity, Roger would experience a more normal emotional state, family life, and social development. As Mara Selvini-Palazzoli pointed out many years ago (1986), whether the child's behavior is organic or psychological, the family support or lack of support will become either part of the solution, or part of the problem. In Roger's case, it was hoped that Roger could be kept safe and hospitalization avoided. The ongoing assessment of biological versus environmental factors would become increasingly clear over time, as well as the extent that family therapy stages 2 through 4 could become a substitute for medication. If it becomes apparent that a child has a lifelong, recurrent, chronic illness, then the family and patient (in stage 4) would need to address acceptance of that reality.

At the beginning of therapy, especially when there are either dangerous or extremely disruptive behaviors that interfere with normal social development, the therapist is likely to help with instrumental and educational management. This book includes family therapy instrumental methods developed over the last 25 years but, in contrast to previous practice, a more open, collaborative, educational dialogue is preferred with the family.

For example, as in Roger's situation, if it is observed that (1) the child acts, followed by the sequence of (2) the father's being somewhat critical and asking the child to "shape up," followed by (3) the mother's support of the child and criticism of the father, then the family would be made more aware of this sequence of events. How the parents negate each other in problem-solving would be accentuated and clarified. This clarification approach would be different from the original, more secretive interventions by family therapists who would subtly introduce a new patterning or simply try to block one of the parents. The clarification of the parents' sequential response to a child's symptom is a key element of stage 1. The communication difficulties revealed in such clarification are a lead-in to stage 2 boundary and power communication difficulties that frequently occur in addition to the particular surface problem.

Another instrumental method partially derived from hypnosis techniques (Haley, 1967) involves the parents repetitively giving positive instructions on proper behavior. In this case, a parent might say, "Roger, we insist that you control your outbursts and use words to express your anger." Then, more softly: "We love you and it will be important for the rest of your life to be able to express your emotions in a way that helps you." In this parenting method, the parents are taught a basic instrumental parenting principle that if an instruction is repetitively presented without allowing alternate possibilities, such as ultimatums or punishments, the child is more likely to follow the parent's wishes, especially if there is reasonable bonding between the parents and the child. Directions are enhanced by good "bonding" if the parent makes good eye contact and touches the child. Another instrumental method is to tell stories with an ending designed to increase the likelihood of a similar "restorative" ending in the patient or child. Such stories are strategic stories rather than conversational stories. The field of family therapy generally has turned away from such instrumental discipline methods that can be, in the wrong hands, abusive and controlling. The current method seeks a balance between reasonable parental control and an understanding and empathy of the child's underlying emotional state.

On the more environmental end of the biological versus environmental spectrum in this clinical situation, Roger's anxiety after his parents leave dramatically portrays an abandonment or separation anxiety that needs exploration and clarification. This youngster literally described fears of earthquakes and other disasters with separation. The family might be asked to discuss all three family members' concerns about being left and how each person has had similar separation or loss of control experiences.

If possible, experiments duplicating the feeling of separation or aloneness would be conducted during the session as a way to clarify the experiences of abandonment, anxiety, and rage. Such deconditioning and exposure would increase the possibility of mastery. One simple experiment is to have family members close their eyes and imagine being away, and then open their eyes and see that they are back, connected with the family.

For this family, another exploratory clarification project would be to rank the order of the various family members and extended family members in terms of being in control or being out-of-control. Again, as this spectrum is explored within the family, there is an increasing opportunity for each member to have the flexibility of feeling in control or out-of-control rather than being unable to see alternatives. Family therapy offers the opportunity for dialogue between one position and the counter position between family members, while this same polarity is frequently reflected in the internal life of any individual; the externalized manifestation of control versus out-of-control actions could be a beginning step toward internal flexibility and the personality issues of stage 3.

Roger's family illustrates the integration of predominantly instrumental approaches combined with the clarification of expressive-relational methods. During the subsequent stages of therapy, the biological versus environmental dimension would become clearer, and the therapy would lean gradually toward a more exploratory, contextual orientation.

☐ The Lombardi Family

The third clinical example illustrates a family where the environmental family dynamics appeared to be more in the foreground than biological temperament factors, although medication was used. In contrast to the previous two examples, the expressive-relational end of the instrumental versus expressive-relational dimension is emphasized for therapeutic intervention, and the environmental end of the biological versus environmental dimension is emphasized as more foreground. Again, surface issues are considered as a first stage of further family work. In this family, medication was used more to facilitate the therapy process than to treat a biological condition.

> The Lombardi family presented with their daughter, Carol, who was a high school senior. The parents were primarily concerned that Carol was abusing alcohol; they were also worried about future educational planning with the view that perhaps Carol should not go to college.
>
> It became clear in the initial sessions that the father had an extremely connected relationship with Carol. During our sessions, the father sat close to her and frequently touched her while the mother sat toward the side.

Although the father was critical of Carol's use of alcohol, he was willing to buy drinks for her at restaurants even though she was underage, and was willing to serve her alcohol at home. In other areas, including the use of money, the father was also unconsciously giving his child mixed messages, for example, wanting her to limit and control herself but modeling opposite behaviors. The family included two children; the older son was described as being successful and "normal." The family described Carol as being "irresponsible." The initial therapy included mediation across the generation gap. That is, in summarizing conversations, the parents were represented as wanting safety and a reasonable propriety for their daughter, and the daughter was represented as needing and wanting freedom and a plan of emancipation from the family. The parents explained further that in Italian families virginity was expected until marriage.

Prozac was used for a 6-month period to help stabilize the teenager's emotional state, and the diagnosis of a mild depression was presented to help the father be more sympathetic and less explosive with the daughter. The family romance dynamics were openly discussed. The idea was presented openly to the family that the daughter in a sense was protecting the marriage by having the parents, and especially the father, focus on the daughter rather than the marriage. Through the daughter, the father appeared to be discussing his concerns about sexuality and aging with the wife.

The parents eventually allowed their daughter to go out of state to college, and marital sessions were held after the daughter left home. In the initial therapy, the focus was on Carol's drinking, the family's responses, and the meaning and messages of Carol's behavior (stage 1). These beginning issues gradually led to fuller discussions of general family patterns, style conflicts, and how Carol would leave home (stages 2–4).

The Lombardi family was helped to deal with the surface emancipation-related symptoms of their daughter. The symptoms appeared to be largely based on environmental family dynamics, although there may have been an element of depression and emotional impulsivity in the daughter. It could also be said that the father had some mild indicators of depression and impulsivity, but medications were not used for him. Basically, clarification, understanding how the family was reluctant to move onto the next stage of emancipation development, and a clarification of the symptoms as protection of the marriage seemed to help the family create their own changes toward life-cycle development.

Cultural and gender issues were also discussed as the context for the presenting symptoms. The basic principle is to include gender and culture issues at each stage of therapy in addition to consideration as a special topic in stage 4.

This case illustrates the evolution of paradoxical interventions. The original family-therapy use of paradoxical intervention was presented in the 1970's. In the Lombardi family, Carol's symptoms could be interpreted as deflecting attention away from her father's anxieties and loss, and if she were to give up these symptoms, he would have to face his marriage difficulties and insecurities. In paradoxical methods, the reverse psychology would be presented: for example, it would be better for the youngster to "sacrifice her life" rather than risk marital discord. In a modification of reverse psychology methods, the dynamics of paradoxical therapies are mentioned and sometimes even the history of that technique is given. The family openly discusses the risks of the daughter changing or not changing, and the risks and repercussions of the family allowing emancipation or not. In the author's method, the situation would be openly discussed by the therapist as follows: "Perhaps you will have difficulty living in an empty nest if the father and mother have to focus on each other instead of focusing on Carol's alcohol abuse and possible sexuality." There would also be discussions about how the parents themselves emancipated and how they hope the daughter will not repeat their mistakes.

☐ The Fitzgerald Family

In this next clinical example, the environmental end of the biological versus environmental dimension is again emphasized. Regarding the instrumental versus expressive-relational dimension, a therapeutic conversation is held between the father (instrumental) and the mother (expressive-relational), with the expressive-relational aspects openly encouraged as an antidote to the father's overly instrumental approach. No psychopharmacology is used.

The Fitzgerald family is currently in the first stage of therapy. This family demonstrates that it is important in family therapy to fully explore the presenting problems, rather than jump too quickly to stages 2 through 4 of therapy.

> A pediatrician referred the family because the 10-year-old, Dawn, was crying in his office about how the parents, especially the father, were "always yelling." The first session included both parents, Dawn, and a 2-year-old sister. The parents, especially the father, were upset because they wanted Dawn to have productive activities even though it was summer vacation, and Dawn said she wanted "to relax and do nothing for awhile." In addition, the father was concerned that she was eating pancakes and other food that he thought was unhealthy. Dawn complained that not only would her father yell at her, but that the parents would yell at each other. She also complained that they paid more attention to the 2-year-old than to her. The mother pointed out that in the sequence of events the father would usually yell and then she would become the "advocate" for Dawn.

The parents prided themselves in focusing on the children and discussed gender roles in our society; they discussed their good feelings about having the mother stay at home to mother the children rather than seek employment. The father also pointed out that he was pleased with this parenting arrangement and described how he had chosen a job where he could stay in town rather than travel.

In the original family group meeting, Dawn was an attractive, articulate girl who made very good personal contact. She was doing well in school and had numerous friends. Basically, the parents had done an excellent job, and it appeared that her crying and complaining in the pediatrician's office, although significant, was also a "ticket of admission," so the parents could eventually deal with their marital issues and perhaps the father could deal with his anger. The father acknowledged that his own father had been intimidating in parenting and that even though he tried not to duplicate his history, he appears to do so automatically. The father had an unusual stare and a somewhat odd void expression. I found myself wondering whether his temperament or difficulty with anger might have some biological component.

This situation illustrates one advantage of family work, that this father eventually may be able to participate in therapy to make his parenting more flexible and be less influenced by the way he was raised. Fathers like Dawn's frequently never reach a therapist unless the family, in this case the 10-year-old daughter, is seen as needing help. The plan, begun in the first session, was to heighten awareness of the parenting phenomena and how Dawn needed help in appreciating the lessons that the parents were trying to teach. Although experiments would be considered to clarify, and perhaps modify, the discipline/teacher role versus the advocate role, it was clear that the family was self-motivated to explore their own issues without extensive directives on the author's part. The therapy "directiveness" would be to enhance awareness of the parental conflict. In addition, individual sessions for Dawn were planned.

While exploring surface issues with the Fitzgerald family, I anticipated stages 2, 3, and 4 of therapy. The organization of the family was overly father-dominated. The communication issues in stage 2 would include correcting the lack of listening and the lack of conversational dialogue. Also, the natural need to take care of the 2-year-old sister had led to the 10-year-old, Dawn, feeling left out. In stage 3, the marital issues would be explored on a deeper personality level, and it was likely that the father's narcissistic issues would need to be made less rigid. As he tried to impose lessons of nutrition and productivity, he demonstrated a characterological sense of righteousness and missionary zeal that had led to alienation rather than acceptance of his ideas. This interpersonal dynamic would likely also take place in the marriage, with the wife excessively needing to please and be accommodating. The couple would also deal with the problems of having children 8 years apart. In stage 3, three-generational interviews with all four grandparents would be included, helping to clarify personality dynamics (see Framo 1992). (The grandparents would be included in stage 1 or 2 if they were an active daily part of the family life.) Another potential issue in stage 4, since the couple focused so exclusively on parenting, would be the nature of the marriage experience and what the wife would do after the children left.

The process of family diagnosis is an evolving one, but it is important in the first stage of therapy to tentatively decide together with the family to what extent the problems need immediate change and to what extent the problems are environmental versus biological. In the Fitzgerald family, the overall treatment approach resonated more readily with the mother, who tried to be understanding and an advocate for Dawn. She also described herself as concerned about feelings and the quality of relationships. Although the father discussed his wish for a warm family feeling and the development of his daughter, he initially appeared predominantly concerned about discipline, behavioral control, and addressing practical problems in the family. The initial therapeutic dilemma was to make sufficient contact with the father so that he would feel that the ultimate result would be in his best interest, that is, for him to be more influential with the daughter and for the daughter to have a more gratifying life.

It was important to delay and extend the first phase of therapy sufficiently to allow a therapy alliance to develop around the needs of the 10-year-old. Although the crux of the eventual family therapy would probably be marital therapy and personality therapy, the family used the daughter to introduce these topics. It was crucial to validate and understand the family's concerns about the child sufficiently so that the entrees to stages 2, 3, and 4 of the therapy would be possible.

The integration process in stage 1 comes from mediating between the instrumental and expressive-relational forces within the family and mediating between the biological versus nonbiological points of view. In addition, the therapist makes an independent diagnostic evaluation of the same dimensional elements. To assure a therapeutic alliance, the therapist initially joins the existing dominant theme, whether it is instrumental or expressive-relational on the one hand, or biological versus environmental on the other. The ultimate goal of the therapy is to introduce a flexible, balanced point of view integrating the polarities of each spectrum. The problem-solving phase of therapy is presented to the family as part of a four-stage model and helps the family think along a spectrum of complexity, rather than having an overly simplistic, surface problem-solving view.

☐ [1]Comparative Therapies for an Itch

In this next section, regarding a personal symptom of the author's (Resnikoff, 1992), the challenge is to integrate therapeutic methods from 20 years ago with contemporary biological and behavioral deconditioning therapies for Stage 1 therapy.

While in my residency training, I, like most trainees, imagined that I had every malady that I read or heard about. I had been suffering from chronic itching near my left forehead hairline for years. I could clearly recall the first appearance of the symptoms, which occurred during a high school math class. In light of what I had learned in psychiatric training, I couldn't help but wonder: Had I been so maternally deprived that I was regressing to autoerotic or autistic stimulation? Was I so narcissistic that I needed external stimulation to remind myself where my boundaries were? Was I engaged in a masturbatory equivalent, especially since my skin irritation sometimes went along with hair twirling and could be soothing? Was I really masochistic and self-mutilating, expressing my aggression in an autistic way, since at times I would scratch this itch? Was I identifying with my critical father, who perhaps was jealous of my special relationship as the youngest of three sons with my mother? Was I having a teenage identity crisis? Interestingly, as I was ruminating about all of these possibilities, the spot felt more irritable and I scratched it more. To my dismay, I gradually found myself with a chronic localized hairline sore.

After some time in private practice, I sought out several different therapies, ostensibly for the training involved, but leaving myself open to opportunities to gain personal insights along the way. Although I was not seeking help specifically for my "picking" habit, it was a clear-cut psychosomatic symptom and lent itself to easy presentation in various therapeutic settings. I sought four different nonbiological approaches using various orientations, all dealing with this symptom, and in the process I experienced some of the therapeutic approaches then available. The approaches are:

1. gestalt therapy
2. psychoanalysis
3. the redecision approach (transactional analysis and gestalt)
4. the strategic hypnotic approach.

At the time, I did not consider pharmacological or behavioral deconditioning methods. Although I have had other contacts with various

---

[1]From *Voices: The Art and Science of Psychotherapy*, Vol. 16, No. 3 (Fall, 1980). With permission of the American Academy of Psychotherapists.

therapists in varied settings, this initial discussion will be limited to these four specific approaches for purposes of clarity.

First, a little background on my symptom. I have bitten and picked my nails as far back as I can remember and carved up a school desk on a regular basis in the first grade. My actual hairline itching and scratching began as I became worried about my math performance in high school. Worries about college or medical school exams exacerbated irritation, as would my trying to concentrate on reading.

Gestalt Therapy

My contact with gestalt therapy included a 3-year postgraduate training and supervisory program with Erving and Miriam Polster. Personal work was included as part of the training program, partly for demonstration purposes. Usually I joined a group of eight trainees in the leaders' living room. When I was the focus, it was either because I had asked to be the focus of the group's attention or because my reactions to others led to my being the focus.

The major goal of the Polsters' therapy was to promote awareness of current perceptions, first within the individual, and later in the individual's contact with others. Group members could also try out new behaviors with each other or dramatize a conflict.

In my case, Erv Polster promoted awareness by instructing me: "Instead of trying to decrease the itch, close your eyes and give special concentration to this sensation." Interestingly, paying more attention without touching lessened the irritability of my skin problem; the therapist then suggested that I could allow my skin itching to join other sensations in my body rather than remaining an isolated symptom. At one point the therapist, typically sharing his own reactions to patient work, sat with me intensely imagining and experiencing what it felt like to be itchy. He shared with the rest of the group the excitement of the sensation.

For further personal contact on one occasion, I was asked to either pick or soothe physically (since the symptom seemed to encompass both polarities) the therapist's hand instead of myself, depending on my sensations. My self-contained ("retroflexive") activity changed into an interpersonal touching communication.

In addition, when I felt the urge to pick I was asked to convey this message in words rather than pick on myself. (For example, saying, "I don't understand" to another person rather than picking on myself). Also, being asked to show the "picked" area to the group revealed my embarrassment about the symptom and provided another contact medium leading to new understanding about my fears of criticism and rejection.

A further experiment with the group included my verbally "picking" on various people's faults. This was quite easy to do in my mind but less easy to do face-to-face. The issue of picking on myself became quite obvious at that point.

The Polsters were experts at finding the positive element to any problem. At times this took the form of finding how a particular activity or symptom was developmentally, if not currently, useful. My picking was positively compared to being highly discriminatory. To further reveal the psychological polarities of "picking," I recall having an experimental dialogue between my discriminating, preoccupied, picky side (characteristics I associated with my father) and the nondiscriminating, self-interested side (more similar to my mother). My picking and being discriminatory was seen as a problem only when taken to an extreme.

The Polsters' approach emphasized discovery of potential messages included in the sensation of itching, as well as enacting these discoveries right at that precise moment during therapy. Understanding the early roots of my symptom flowed naturally from this discovery process. The therapy emphasized the potential symbolic messages that the sensation of itching conveyed both to me (for example, my need to be soothed or criticized) and toward others (for example, wanting to confront or pick at them).

The Psychoanalytic Approach

I have completed 5 years of four-session-per-week traditional psychoanalytic therapy. The psychiatrist, Peter Manjos, was well recognized in his field but was less well-known nationally compared to the Polsters. Again, as in the other approaches, the itching symptom was only a small focus of the total experience. In psychoanalytic work, my free-floating thoughts to various aspects of the itching sensation were crucial, as well as how I imagined my therapist to be reacting to a person who would have such a symptom. In some detail, we explored how I even "pick" on myself for having a pick. Instead of simply condemning myself for what I had labeled "preoedipal" or "oedipal" behavior, I was encouraged to accept all the various aspects of my character as being me—not something to be diagnosed, otherwise pigeonholed, or discarded.

As with my symptom, my therapist was attributed with picky as well as soothing maternal qualities. At other times he seemed to be perfect (like I imagined my father to be), very powerful (like I imagined my mother to be), or incompetent (also attributed to my mother). My picking was associated with all three qualities, either related to my frustration about not being all-knowing and omnipotent, or related to the anxiety about feeling helpless.

Compared to the gestalt approach, there was less instruction on how to develop fantasies and fewer formal experiments to facilitate the process of understanding the roots of my symptom. The basic format, however, encouraged discussion of my thoughts and feelings toward the therapist. Before beginning analysis I envisioned spending endless tedious hours intellectualizing about my past. Instead, focusing on my frustrations and admiration regarding the therapist, as well as letting my mind wander, led to a fascinating "present" experience.

The frequent and long-term nature of the therapy gave importance to everyday matters and gave me time to internalize a positive, analyzing mental set as opposed to a picky, destructive mental set.

Redecision Therapy (TA-Gestalt)

This approach emphasizes analyzing the early developmental decisions a child makes—decisions that still operate actively in adult life, often without one's awareness. Redecision work thus attempts to activate the feelings that were involved in making that original decision, and then using adult awareness in redeciding what is—or was—needed to solve an old problem that is still causing conflict. I got to know redecision work in a 50-hour contact with Bob and Mary Goulding, who have a national reputation in transactional analysis and redecision therapy.

After hearing the description of my symptom and understanding the comforting, as well as the aggressive aspects of my skin problem, Bob Goulding suggested a preverbal experiment. I had mentioned at one point that my mother had always insisted that she had to get dentures because all of her calcium had gone into milk to breastfeed my brothers and me. To experience the guilt and anger of feeling that I had somehow hurt my mother by breastfeeding, Goulding told me to fantasize and then enact (physically and with sounds) biting her breast. To my surprise, this was a very emotional experience for me. Afterwards, the therapist had me choose a nurturing woman in the group to comfort me. The redecision that took place was that if my mother felt bad about "sacrificing" her milk, I could redecide not to feel guilty about it. That was her problem, not mine.

In videotape work with the Gouldings, I saw that the left side of my face (on which the itching was localized) was more immobile than the right side. The right side would reveal grimaces, smiles, and frowns, while the left side was relatively still. This fact seemed to provide personal evidence for split-brain phenomena; that is, my left-sided symptom seemed to be an attempt to stimulate that side to include more emotional and personal contact.

Strategic, Hypnotic Therapy

For this therapeutic approach I visited Milton Erickson in Scottsdale, Arizona, for 2 days. I was attracted to Erickson because of our mutual interest in family therapy. I was also interested in strategies of problem-solving therapy, especially for use in the early phases of therapy. The therapist was perhaps doing much more than I was aware of, but here are some of the things I think happened. First, while in a hypnotic state and at the therapist's suggestion, I was able to recreate beautiful, enjoyable experiences from my childhood, such as lounging around Cedar Brook Pond feeding the ducks. While I was under hypnosis, I was told to focus on a bouquet of lavender flowers in front of me; the therapist simply said that in the future when I was feeling like picking, I could think of lavender flowers instead.

The underlying process, I think, was to condition my previous positive childhood memories at the pond (symbolized by lavender flowers), together with my current negative symptom—the picking. Erickson stated over and over again that the power to solve problems comes from the client's own psyche and experience; the hypnotist simply helps develop the process of using this power. My power in this instance was the ability to appreciate a beautiful pond and recall this beauty.

Milton Erickson is also known for his storytelling ability, which he apparently used to give indirect suggestions to avoid patient reluctance about change. Erickson seemed to feel that a part of my self-picking was a frustrated wish for fame. He described his own experience of trying to enjoy activities for themselves, rather than always anticipating what might result from them in the future. The suggestion to me was obvious. Erickson also used his well-known food stories about how two people with different gastronomic preferences could each enjoy a meal in their own way. The client (in this case, the author) was left to find what might apply. I could easily apply the idea of being less harsh on myself as well as enjoying what "food" (job, sex, money) is available (without hateful envy).

Reviewing these four experiences, what struck me was that they were all different but all useful. The Polsters' gestalt approach, similar to the developmental dimension of family stages in this book, worked from surface experiences and metaphors to deeper meanings and personality issues. Instrumental techniques were used for awareness, not for correction of symptoms. The psychoanalytic approach emphasized personality issues and family interpersonal dynamics from childhood and moved quickly from surface free associations to stage 2 and stage 3 issues. In Goulding redecision therapy, surface concerns were also quickly connected with stage 3 personality dynamics, where redecisions were used to expand early perceptions. In Ericksonian hypnosis, the focus remained on the surface symptom, with efforts to modify the picking through relaxation.

This personal example illustrates the variety of emphases possible regarding surface issues before boundary, personality, and life transitional issues are considered. For family work, the usual mistake is to move too quickly away from surface issues before a beginning therapeutic alliance can be established.

Biological/Behavioral Approaches

How can these earlier approaches be integrated with current research and clinical practice in treating skin picking and trichotillomania (hair twirling and pulling), as well as other repetitive movement behaviors or thoughts that appear to be involuntary?

In the last 15 years, there has been an explosion in the biological understanding of obsessive-compulsive phenomena and the obsessive-compulsive disorder clinical spectrum. Crucial research work has been done by Baxter (Baxter et al., 1987) and expanded in a book by Schwartz, *Brainlock* (1995). Basically, on PET metabolism brain scans, it appears that the caudate nucleus is overactive in obsessive-compulsive disorder (OCD). It is important to emphasize that OCD is distinctive because it includes repetitive thoughts (such as counting or repeating words) and actions (such as repetitive handwashing) that have no obvious secondary gain or pleasurable satisfaction. These thoughts and actions are experienced as nonproductive and alien and yet seem to protect the patient from underlying fears such as contamination or AIDS. The author's skin picking habit would not be a "pure" compulsion since there is an element of pleasure. The picking could also be considered a tic.

An interesting finding, in line with the theme of this book, is that *both* psychological behavioral therapy and serotonin-enhancing drug therapy are beneficial in helping obsessions and compulsions and normalizing the PET scans. Behavioral methods alone can be as effective as psychopharmacology. If anything, behavioral control that exposes the fears or anxieties that occur when obsessions or compulsions are controlled provides for longer lasting results than medications (Greist, 1995).

Susan Swedo (Swedo, Leonard, Garvey, Mittleman, Allen, Perlmutter, Dow, Zamkoff, Dubbert, & Collgee, 1998) has implicated streptococcus infection as a cause of childhood OCD. Her research provides a clear example of biological disease leading to behavioral problems. In another new biological concept, neurosurgeons have inserted electrodes in the thalamic region of the brain to help regulate movement disorders. In considering the integration of biology and functional psychology, it is interesting to speculate that repetitive behaviors and thoughts are generally adaptive for mastery of life's challenges, but under certain abnormal states become excessive (see Jensen et al., 1997).

Over the last decade there have been two phases in considering biological treatment approaches to skin picking and trichotillomania. In the early 90's, when psychiatry seemed obsessed with OCD behavioral control, medications for obsessive-compulsive disorder including Anafranil (an older tricyclic antidepressant that increases serotonin) and serotonin-enhancing agents (SSRIs) were seen as being the curative answer. It has become clearer over time that skin picking and trichotillomania are somewhat different from the purer obsessive-compulsive illness, and psychopharmacology has been less successful than previously thought. Skin picking and trichotillomania can also be seen as a tic-like phenomena of Tourette's syndrome. The current instrumental treatment for surface compulsions or obsessions is behavioral deconditioning, either alone or in combination with serotonin-enhancing agents. The target goal is 50–75% control; in a way, it is important for the client not to be too obsessive about controlling the obsessions and compulsions.

In contemporary neuropsychiatric thinking, the author's itching and picking would be considered part of the OCD spectrum (see McElroy, Phillips, & Keck, 1994) that includes OCD, Tourette's Syndrome, and certain other neurological movement disorders. Obsessive compulsive disorder and Tourette's are considered part of a spectrum because of a familial association and similar repetitive behaviors, even though the specific pathological brain anatomy and medications for treatment are different. Obsessive-compulsive disorder with unwanted repetitive thoughts and actions is clearly different from the obsessive-compulsive personality, where interpersonal control is sought after. Classic OCD behaviors include excessive, repetitive handwashing and rituals, such as checking repetitively to avoid dirt and contamination (for example, with AIDS). Tourette's syndrome is characterized by involuntary, repetitive tics, movements, or vocalizations. Risperdal is the current medication treatment. Attention deficit disorder with hyperactivity, bipolar depression, and anxiety are frequently associated with OCD and Tourette's, making the clinical picture quite complex. Further complicating treatment, stimulants that can treat hyperactivity often make tics worse; also, serotonin enhancing agents used for OCD can worsen bipolar conditions.

Arguing against the OCD spectrum concept, Neal Swerdlow (1999) has emphasized the distinction of OCD and tics. Although the OCD spectrum has common elements of repetitive actions and thoughts, together with hereditary associations and comorbid associations with bipolar illness, ADHD, and anxiety, tics have a separate neuroanatomical basis and a different response to psychopharmacology. The "lumpers" would see the author's picking problems as part of the OCD spectrum without distinguishing tics from OCD. The "splitters" would try to precisely identify a brain etiology and treatment. I prefer the "lumper" philosophy, since my intent throughout this book is to build connections and bridges, whether with symptoms, personality characteristics, or schools of thought.

Behaviorists would have me be "exposed" to the anxiety of not picking. The trend in psychiatry is to emphasize instrumental medications or instrumental cognitive/behavioral controls for surface symptoms. The inclusive, integrative model presented here includes these instrumental methods in conjunction with the expressive-relational interpersonal awareness and support described in the environmental methods.

Current psychiatric treatment still emphasizes the instrumental combination of medication and behavioral therapies, but the pendulum appears to be swinging back somewhat to emphasize quality-of-life issues of the whole person with a neurological problem, rather than emphasizing illness. John Walkup (1999; Walkup & Riddle, 1996), for example, has an integrated approach for OCD and tic disorders that emphasizes parental education, the need for development of special interests and character, separate from the illness, and a deemphasis on medication. Walkup points out that many childhood tics decrease at about the age of 20 and that children need to think of themselves as "special" in ways other than their tics. Walkup's methods are predominantly instrumental rather than psychodynamic or narrative expressive-relational.

In my situation, I am aware that my own fingernail picking and skin picking, although still somewhat present, can be at a very low level for months or even years until a stressful situation occurs. I, like many of the participants in research projects, have not used medications to control my symptoms. Also, interestingly in a book primarily regarding interpersonal and family therapies, most people with obsessions and compulsions keep these symptoms private or secret. To the extent that family members can be included in the awareness of the symptoms and be part of the support structure for change, the family and family therapy can be a resource. It is still difficult in contemporary practice to evaluate to what extent a picking or trichotillomania symptom is biological or, instead, a symptom of environmental anxiety, an autoerotic stimulant, or an impulse directed inward instead of outward (retroflection). Interestingly, the original therapy insights that I described in my postgraduate experiences are still valid and perhaps especially so as biology and psychopharmacology are integrated with other psychotherapeutic constructs.

Obsessive-compulsive disorder repetitive thoughts and behavior symptoms can be part of any other clinical picture whether it is depression, anxiety, schizophrenia, perfectionism, or normal personality functioning.

In several clinical family situations that come to mind, the obsessive-compulsive disorder component that included rituals, preoccupations, or in one case trichotillomania, became apparent only after the presenting problems and family issues were being addressed. The choice of using medication or behavioral approaches, and considering the importance of the obsessive-compulsive symptom in the larger family interpersonal picture would all be subjects for family discussion.

In summary, the exploration of presenting problems for the family involves the spectrum of biological versus environmental issues and the spectrum of changing versus exploring and clarifying the presenting problem. The previous historical use of manipulative techniques and efforts to control symptoms are presented to the family for consideration and collaboration, with an open explanation of the intent of any therapeutic experiments.

The five clinical examples illustrate the psychopharmacology/family therapy interface in treating surface symptoms. In treating Jack's bipolar manic delusions, collaboration of the mother's spiritual and father's practical approaches was needed to support the medication. In controlling Roger's self-destructive biologically mediated impulses, medication was needed before family system separation anxiety and self-regulatory concerns could be addressed. Carol's high school drinking and sexuality were considered as symptoms reflecting marital difficulties and separation issues. Prozac, however, facilitated the treatment of these surface concerns. Dawn's complaints about being unhappy in the midst of parental yelling were taken very seriously, without the help of medication, as an entrée to marital and personality problems in the parents. Medication would probably be useful at a later stage of therapy for the father's temperament. With the author's picking behavior, the challenge was to incorporate newer biological and behavioral deconditioning knowledge and methods regarding the OCD spectrum with older psychotherapy methods that offer a combination of instrumental control and expressive-relational insights and support, including interpersonal implications.

If a therapist is successful in considering the presenting problem seriously and respectfully, whether in an instrumental or relational way, the family will feel heard and understood. This sense of security is essential before the family will be able to productively delve into deeper issues. Also, once the family and therapist have reduced the family's initial suffering, contextual issues that contributed to that suffering can be addressed more directly. The therapeutic alliance is bolstered by the effectiveness of stage 1 success. Chapters 4–6 will focus on stages 2, 3, and 4 as they usually emerge in family therapy: communication, personality, and life transitions/spirituality concerns.

Stage 2 Therapy: What are the Organizational and Communication Difficulties in the Family? How are Boundaries and Power Regulated?

While the family and therapist are considering the family's initial complaints and suffering, the structural organization of the family becomes apparent along a continuum of strong leadership to weak leadership and a continuum of closeness and distance. How the family positions or describes itself reflects these organizational properties. Families in treatment often have rigid leadership or lack of leadership, and rigid closeness and distancing arrangements. How family members look at, hear, touch, or talk to each other is foreground in stage 2 of family therapy.

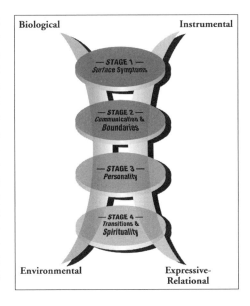

As in all stages of therapy, especially when considering psychophar-macology, the family discusses biological versus environmental issues in correcting communication and organizational problems. In addition, the family and therapist decide whether or not immediate change is needed.

☐ The Cohesiveness/Adaptability Diagram

David Olson (Olson, Spronkle, & Russell, 1979; Olson, 1986) has devel-oped a cohesiveness/adaptability model to describe family boundaries and power, which is considered especially useful because his spectrum con-cepts mirror the dimensional emphasis for integration that have been proposed here. On the horizontal axis, Olson describes families that are extremely close and emotionally involved ("enmeshed") at one end of the dimension, and families whose members are distant and isolated from each other ("isolated"), at the other end. This axis is also referred to as the low-boundary versus high-boundary dimension.

On the vertical axis, Olson describes a dimension of power and or-ganizational control. On the upper end of the axis is extreme control, "dictatorship," and directive power; on the lower end of the axis are the more nondirective, "anarchical" styles of family leadership. This axis can be called the high-power versus low-power dimension.

The Olson diagram can be used to describe individual family members or the style of the family as a whole. One theory is that, as our society becomes more technological and impersonal, families are moving more toward the isolated, anarchy quadrant of Olson's diagram.

☐ Juan and Margaret

The first clinical example illustrates a couple with the husband's directive control and closeness matched with the wife's opposite nondirective and distant qualities. The cultural and ethnic differences are polarized, and gender issues are also in conflict. Pharmacotherapy is used to create a boundary experiment.

> Juan, a Latino professional, fell instantly in love and in lust with a somewhat younger statuesque woman, Margaret, who was from England. Juan was outspoken and overly involved and controlling with Margaret's thoughts, emotions, and behaviors. He felt he had the right to dominate. Margaret had a tendency to avoid conflict and confrontation. She was a person of few words and it was difficult to know what she was thinking or feeling.
>
>   The therapy, intermittent over a 4-year period, has helped Juan have more respect for boundaries and differences and has allowed Margaret to

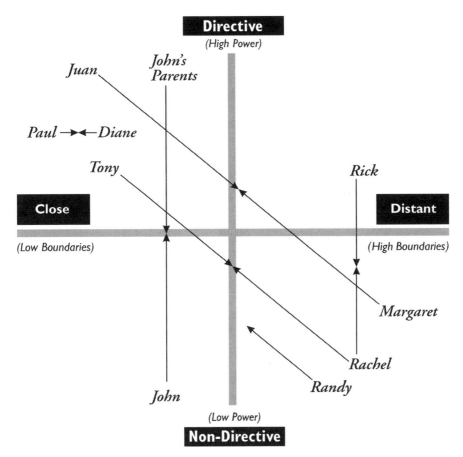

FIGURE 4.1. In the cohesiveness/adaptability diagram, clinical examples are placed to illustrate how closeness versus distance and directive versus nondirective rigidities can be clarified and then changed to a more flexible arrangement. The "instrumental" quadrant is directive/distant; the "expressive-relational" quadrant is nondirective/close.

be more sturdy and assertive. This couple conceptualized their boundary issues as both gender-based and culturally based. Juan explained that as a Mexican man he was trained to say what he thought even if it included vulgarity and confrontation. Juan felt that this expressiveness was a "macho thing" and that men were more inclined to this style than women. Both Juan and Margaret conceptualized the wife's propriety and distancing as being an English cultural trait. Margaret felt that women in general were more likely than men to try to smooth over difficulties and maintain peace and harmony.

Historically, Juan dealt with anxieties in his childhood family by being aggressive and proactive. Margaret had the opposite reaction to stress in her upbringing—she would withdraw. In one session, the couple visually demonstrated their body language boundaries with Juan aggressively bullying his way, with fists. Margaret held her hands and arms up to shield herself from danger. These body language boundary reactions had been lifelong adaptations to stressful circumstances.

In therapy, Margaret used Prozac for menstrual irritability and difficulty in negotiating her wants and needs. This medication helped Margaret stay involved in confrontational conversations instead of leaving the scene, and it also eased her problems with clarity and forcefulness. As part of a therapeutic barter, Juan agreed to take low doses of Inderal, a beta-blocker, to control his temper outbursts and create appropriate distance when requested by Margaret.

Juan is in the directive/close quadrant, and Margaret is in the nondirective/distant quadrant, of the Olson diagram. The family therapist can either help clarify the boundary and power dimensions in the family explicitly and wait for spontaneous change, or the therapist can direct experiments to create fluid movement along the dimensions and create flexible boundaries and power arrangements. These same concepts have been discussed in systems terms, where family members are seen as operating primarily with their psychological "gates open" or their psychological "gates closed." The therapeutic goal is to create a flexible gate depending on the situation.

James Alexander (Alexander & Parsons, 1982) has promoted the clinical concept of initially joining with the family's boundary and power organization. Then, in small incremental steps, changes are introduced that at first still preserve the family's organization. For example, communication may be clarified or improved between overly enmeshed pairs, but no attempt would be made to create an "interpersonal divorce" in such pairs. With Juan and Margaret, the therapy alliance initially joined the male-dominated system, and then took incremental steps toward balancing the power and boundary arrangements. The therapy method included humorous confrontations to accentuate and characterize the boundary and power positions. It was suggested that Juan and Margaret would change "when they were ready." This classification along power and boundary dimensions clarified the power and boundary conflicts for Juan and Margaret and helped lead them away from their polarized positions.

Psychopharmacology for Boundary Regulation

Using the *Diagnostic and Statistical Manual of Mental Disorders* (DSM) (1994) for diagnoses, one finds that certain diagnoses of surface symptoms (Axis I) would more likely create emotional distancing, while others would create a blur in the boundaries. In this chapter the emphasis is on the boundary effect (stage 2) rather than the symptom itself (stage 1). Appropriate use of psychopharmacology not only addresses symptoms, but also helps regulate normal boundary functioning. For example, youngsters or adults with ADHD, schizophrenic thought disorders, anxiety disorders, or OCD traits are preoccupied with their own symptoms and out of touch with others. Ritalin for ADHD, Risperdal, Zyprexa, or Seroquel for schizophrenia, Zoloft or Paxil for anxiety, and Zoloft, Paxil, or Anafranil for obsessive-compulsive illness facilitate therapy and promote greater closeness, intimacy, and communication, both within the family and for therapy.

At the opposite end of the continuum, certain kinds of depression, bipolar illness, or severe borderline symptomatology usually create boundary invasions and excessive dependency or control. Antidepressants such as Wellbutrin or Prozac for depression, Depakote or Lithium for bipolar illness, and Zoloft or Paxil combined with anticonvulsants such as Depakote for impulse control, help contain boundary invasions and again make interpersonal communication and boundary regulation more flexible.

Personality styles (discussed in the next chapter) can create interpersonal distance or closeness as well as directive or nondirective interactions. For example, paranoid or narcissistic personalities would likely be controlling and power hungry, while dependent schizoid individuals would likely be the opposite. Schizoid or narcissistic personality disorders would lead to distancing, while borderline, histrionic, or dependent personality features would lead to overcloseness. Pharmacology can be an adjunct for working with personality disorders, helping to create flexible, more appropriate contact and organization within the family.

Just as a kiss can result in more closeness *or* more distance depending on the reaction of the recipient, the interactional sequence would be important in each diagnostic situation described above. For example, if one family member were aggressive and abusive, one would expect distancing. However, if another family member is inclined to rescue or is drawn to such behavior, an increasingly close interaction can result.

With Juan and Margaret, medications were used to create more flexible boundaries. For Juan, Inderal helped contain his invasive, controlling anger and helped to create more distance. In a complementary way, Margaret's Prozac during menstrual times helped her to articulate her thoughts and complaints rather than being overly reactive and distancing; medication was used for temperament modification as it affected boundaries, rather than for any diagnosable condition.

☐ Rachel and Rick; Rachel and Tony

The next clinical example again illustrates boundary and power interpersonal issues with an emphasis on family history patterning. The use of therapy "experiments" is discussed, with an emphasis on enhancing accurate and empathic interpersonal contact. Medications were not prescribed for these couples.

> I have been Rachel's therapist intermittently over a 6-year period. Her first husband, Rick, was a compulsive athlete and worker. He had a controlling nature and told Rachel, for example, that she should not drive to her best friend's wedding because there would be too much traffic. Unfortunately, Rachel did not go to the wedding. Rachel generally complied with Rick's mandates, even though he was extremely emotionally distant. In her own upbringing, Rachel had decided to be independent and very distant from her family in response to what she perceived as the overemotionality and control of her mother. The marriage ended when Rick insisted on an abortion and Rachel refused.
>
> Rachel married a second time to an Italian man, Tony, who, compared to her first husband, is emotionally involved and possessive. Tony controls with guilt, as opposed to the cognitive reasoning her first husband used. The effect is that when Tony insists on family or other communal group participation, Rachel rebels and becomes distant and oppositional. In therapy, Rachel has been given rituals, at times to comply with her husband, and at other times to control her space and time. These alternating periods of closeness and distance have been negotiated with her husband and have led to greater boundary flexibility.

Rachel is in the distant/nondirective Olson quadrant. Her first husband, Rick, was in the distant/directive quadrant. The second husband is in the close/directive quadrant.

Bowlby (1969) outlined two main interpersonal bonding patterns in life. To illustrate this clinical closeness versus distance dichotomy, Bowlby told a story about a child and a mother who are both sitting on a park bench, both feeling anxious. In the first scenario, the child cuddles with the mother and does not leave. In the second scenario, the opposite extreme, the anxious child and mother remain separate from each other. The child plays and stays away from the mother, and the mother stays on the park bench in collusion with this separation.

Bowlby points out that the ideal situation would be for the child to intermittently come back to the mother for "refueling" and then return to playing, separate from the mother. Bowlby's speculation is that these two polarized closeness-versus-distance patterns lead to two major problems in interpersonal relationships throughout life: on the one hand, individuals who create too much interpersonal distance and, on the other hand, individuals who create too much interpersonal closeness. Rachel was painfully aware of her use of distancing as protection and was willing not only to trace the history and patterning of this distancing, but also to experiment with being more engaged and making better contact without being submissive.

Judith Brown (1979) has created a clinical experiment for exploring interpersonal relationship contact elements. These contact elements include:

1. accurate sensory contact
2. projective empathic contact
3. merger and subjective empathy contact.

In a clinical exercise, one member of the couple looks at, listens to, and touches the spouse (or partner) in three separate time periods. During phase one of the visual sensation exercise, for example, the first person describes in a scientific, descriptive, concrete way what he or she sees. In phase two, the first person describes his or her imagination of what the visual cues mean. This is an empathic speculation, such as imagining that visually observed watery eyes means that the partner is sad. In phase three, the first person describes his or her subjective experience of observing and noticing the visual cues. After the three phases of the exercise, the couple discusses the content and process of the experiment before reversing roles.

The surprising clinical finding is how frequently couples or family members confuse speculation with fact, leading to distorted communication and misunderstanding. Therapy helps reveal and correct the blocks to full relationship communication and contact. Rachel overinterpreted Tony's intentions as dangerous and sinister. She had a difficult time sometimes saying "yes" and sometimes saying "no"; Rachel characteristically said no, especially when under stress. Tony had a difficult time accepting that Rachel might occasionally want to say "no." He took Rachel's request for separate time as a personal rejection. Conversations were conducted in therapy to encourage accurate listening, with Rachel clarifying when she was rejecting or criticizing Tony and when she simply needed some time alone. Later, historical patterns regarding closeness and distance were shared. As mentioned above, the contact boundaries between Rachel and Tony became more flexible; both experienced their relationship as increasingly satisfying.

Historically, the main complaint about "structural family therapy" is that the "proper" family organization was imposed by the therapist on the family and frequently by men therapists against women patients (see Minuchin & Fishman, 1981). A contemporary application of boundary and power concepts would be to educate the family as to the historic principles and concepts about "healthy" interpersonal organizational structures, and then to have the family collaboratively consider experiments that would explore possible power and boundary arrangements. This experimentation may include "family psychodrama sculpting," where the family is placed physically in their predominant structure and asked if that matches their perception of the power and closeness arrangements. The experiment can then be designed to consider new options, again mutually with the family.

☐ Paul and Diane

The next example illustrates a couple with both husband and wife demonstrating closeness but also directive and control issues, resulting in violent exchanges. In addition, triangulation issues because of an extramarital affair are discussed. Psychopharmacology is used to help create more distance.

> Paul and Diane, both lawyers, have separated after a long-term marriage with three children. Paul has intercepted Diane's e-mail and burned her clothes; Diane has paraded her new boyfriend provocatively in front of Paul and pointed out the boyfriend's superior qualities. Meetings to discuss child custody arrangements are explosive, with slander and hatred from both sides, usually regarding unmet needs. Diane felt invaded; Paul felt abandoned. The couple is considering a reconciliation emphasizing friendship, without the expectation that the other person will provide relief from lifelong suffering and abuse. Both Paul and Diane have started on Paxil to help reduce the explosive oversensitivity.

This couple illustrates the "symmetrical" marital arrangement, where both husband and wife have similar power and boundary characteristics. The result is blaming arguments and accusations replacing normal conversations and negotiations. The triangulation structure of the affair further provokes the situation. Frank Pittman (1989) has discussed the spectrum of affair effects, all the way from creating boundaries to the opposite result of inciting jealousy and increased interaction. The latter is the case here.

Many authors have viewed triangulation as a nearly universal interpersonal complication; the "villain, victim, and rescuer triangle" is the key issue in numerous books and films, as well as in many family therapy situations. The "third party" can be work, sports, or the computer as well as another person. In stage 2, the boundaries and subgroupings are the focus, rather than the personality styles contributing to the triangulation.

For Diane, the affair reflected a spiritual salvation and relief from suffering that she attributed to gender-related issues. Diane felt abused as a woman in her upbringing, in education, professionally, as a wife, and as a mother. On the other hand, she wanted to preserve her family if possible and felt unable to leave her husband and children. In his book *Intimate Terrorism*, Michael Miller (1995) postulates that there is an ongoing, escalating battle of the sexes in many marriages. Miller describes many wives who have made positive changes in assertiveness and insistence on equality, only to be met with new power maneuvers by husbands.

Paul and Diane were on a rapidly escalating course until they began therapy. Like mediation, the therapy process compartmentalized the emotional, resentment, and power issues from the practical negotiations regarding childcare and financial arrangements. The process of the therapy modeled the boundaries that were needed for civil conversations: one person talking at a time, a no-violence rule, and a no-slander rule.

Paxil was included for both Paul and Diane to facilitate the therapy and negotiation process. It is still unclear if Paul and Diane will reconcile; but because of the author's openly stated bias toward preserving families, because of the history of closeness, and because of the author's belief that couples can learn from marital patterns before considering divorce, delaying the divorce and continuing therapy has been recommended.

☐ John's Family

The next family also illustrates an escalating power struggle, with excessive parental control. The general concept of parents and therapists as consultants versus managers is also discussed.

> The parents of a 3-year-old boy, John, who was refusing to eat and losing weight, brought him in for an evaluation. John had severe medical problems in the first year of life, and his parents were concerned about nutrition and had a preoccupation with food for the youngster; they overly insisted that the child eat. Through therapy, the parents switched their focus to bowel training, ignoring food issues. Even though the parents were overcontrolling with toilet training, the change relieved pressure on the food issue. Also, the parents had more investment in the food issue because of food's relationship to John's earlier health problems.
>
> At the dinner table, the father was assigned the role of complaining about food and saying that he would not eat the mother's cooking (as a way to externalize John's anger and shift the control dynamics). With this shift away from controlling John's food, the power struggle regarding food ended. The youngster began to eat.
>
> Interestingly, the parents had numerous power struggles between themselves and 10 years later the parents divorced, instigated by the wife, when she felt she could no longer tolerate the husband's dominance.

In the Olson diagram, John was in the nondirective position (except through passivity), and the parents were in the directive end of the power continuum.

The discussion of John's family parallels the professional application of power and boundary concepts in clinical family situations. If a therapist presents what is "normal" to a family in a too forceful or too hierarchical manner, the family is likely to rebel without even considering the suggestions. The power politics of families are especially dramatic with teenagers. One useful concept is to have the parents present "recommendations" repetitively without ultimatums or punishments. Frequently, with less control, the teen will consider such recommendations. Similarly, if a therapist suggests experiments or "recommendations," then therapy collaboration is more likely.

The manager-versus-consultant dimension is especially important with psychopharmacology. Families usually consider medications or other suggestions if they are presented with a genuine spirit of caring, kindness, and concern, rather than control. Following the ideas of Erving and Miriam Polster (1999), it is useful for the therapist to view patients as "reluctant" instead of "resistant"; this view helps avoid unnecessary clinical power struggles with families.

☐ Randy's Family

The next clinical example illustrates that the main therapy for a family in which one member is schizophrenic—once initial psychotic symptoms are resolved—should emphasize stage 2 practical interpersonal communication rather than more complex and overstimulating stage 3 and 4 historical and philosophical issues.

> Randy dropped out of the Massachusetts Institute of Technology with one course—quantum physics—to go before graduation. Previously a brilliant math whiz, but socially a loner, Randy had developed delusions. He believed that the O. J. Simpson murder trial was a stunt and was convinced that Nicole Simpson was still alive. Randy returned home and despite anxieties and fears, refused medications.
>
> With the support of Randy's parents, a sister, and regular family therapy meetings, Randy was "protected" from the world and given an apartment near the parents' house. His mother provided food, and Randy occasionally attended basketball games or the poker parlor as the paranoia subsided. A year later Randy experienced another paranoid episode after being stopped by the police for a routine auto violation. After hospitalization, where Randy described a conspiracy and violently refused medication and therapy (with a different psychiatrist), Randy agreed to more regular outpatient family therapy with me as well as medication, although he still claimed that nothing was wrong.
>
> Once Randy started on Zyprexa, 20 mgs per day, and Prozac, 20 mgs per day, for antidelusional and antidepressant effects, there was a dramatic improvement in functioning. Family therapy focused on practical social and communication training. Individual therapy alternated with family meetings. For example, at his sister's wedding, Randy was instructed to "make contact" with guests by saying, "I'm glad you could come; I hope you have a good time," without any obligation to have a more personal, or emotional, conversation. Similarly, as Randy began to apply for computer jobs, he rehearsed being positive rather than negative. He practiced describing his computer skills. Randy also rehearsed how to look, listen, and touch in

appropriate ways during sessions. Using an educational approach, the parents were urged not to be overly harsh about their wishes for Randy to stop smoking cigarettes. I pointed out the research indicating that excessive conflict can increase the chances of a relapse (Anderson, Reiss, & Hogarty, 1986). Randy has just begun a new computer job that, while below his previous level of accomplishment, offers the hope of self-sufficiency and social functioning. Randy says it is too soon to consider women or dating. The parents have begun marital therapy.

This clinical vignette supports the idea that the new atypical antipsychotics for schizophrenia (Clozaril, Zyprexa, Risperdal, and Seroquel) have renewed hopes for beneficial maintenance therapy and family therapy for patients suffering from schizophrenia. The therapeutic work combined with medication helps to create improved communication without the overstimulation of personality or psychodynamic explorations.

This notion has been described by Gerard Hogarty (Hogarty, Kornblith, Greenwald, DiBarry, Cooley, Ulrich, Carter, & Flesher, 1997) as "Personal Therapy." More recently, Hogarty has also described "Cognitive Enhancement Therapy" that uses computers and other training programs previously used after brain trauma, to treat schizophrenic cognition. These programs enhance the missing abstraction ability and reduce the excessive sensitivity and dysregulation noted in distorted schizophrenic cognition (Hogarty & Flesher, 1999). The use of medications has allowed patients such as Randy employment and functional socializing. Family therapy and family support, including education about schizophrenic physical changes, programs, medication, and communication enhancement, can promote this process. For example, families can be educated about the reduced cortical mass and abnormal excessive adolescent "brain connection pruning" in the schizophrenic condition and the characteristic cognitive impairments and social impairments; it can be pointed out that medications help preserve the cortex in (childhood) schizophrenia (see Rapoport, 1999a,b).

In the Olson diagram, Randy is currently in the distant/nondirective quadrant. Therapy and family support are helping him make better interpersonal contact and lower his interpersonal boundaries. Randy has an increasing ability to make changes and has a better sense of directing his professional and personal life. The core personality concerns, such as Randy's mistrustful belief systems, are not given a priority and, in fact, are deemphasized as being overstimulating.

In the biological versus environmental dimension, environmental supports and training, with the help of medications, can help override biologically mediated deficits. Medication, protection from overstimulation, and cognitive retraining are all instrumental approaches. It is important to include basic love, support, and understanding from the expressive-relational point of view, while not primarily relying on such support for healing. Hogarty has reported clear-cut research findings that "personal therapy" and "cognitive enhancement therapy" markedly improve treatment results, compared to medication alone, especially after a 2- to 3-year period.

☐ Dimensional Considerations

In the Olson cohesiveness/adaptability model, the distant/directive quadrant is similar to the instrumental style of creating therapeutic change. The close/nondirective quadrant is similar to the expressive-relational style for therapeutic change. Each end of this continuum has "good news and bad news" possibilities, as illustrated in the clinical examples. The therapeutic goal is a flexible integration of the differing boundary and power styles, plus accurate sensory and empathic interpersonal contact.

All five clinical examples illustrate communication misunderstandings. The power struggles for Juan and Margaret were discussed primarily in a cultural Mexican versus English context. Rachel's developmental patterning with her mother was seen as a major factor in her need for privacy. Paul and Diane discussed both gender struggles and developmental deprivations in describing their violent battles. John's eating difficulties illustrated the frequent temptation for parents or therapists to be overdominating when trying to correct a problem. Randy needed help with interpersonal communication skills once his delusions were under control.

Medications were used both to shore up boundaries and power, and to lower boundaries and power. The first four examples illustrated primarily environmental concerns, with medications used to promote communication rather than to treat target symptoms. The last example with Randy illustrated that communication training can be possible after treating target symptoms with psychopharmacology.

The staging and therapeutic alliance dimension is complex. Paul and Diane, as well as John's family, sought help mostly for power and boundary issues. Most couples or families, like Juan and Margaret as well as Rachel, go through stage 1 surface issues or symptoms before boundary and power concerns become foreground. The progression of therapy is a therapeutic choice to be openly negotiated with the family.

Even though many structural family therapy concepts have been out of favor because of therapeutic overcontrol and imposing the therapist's idea of "normal," such concepts can be valuable to therapists and treatment families, if presented collaboratively and as experiments. Integrating both instrumental and expressive-relational approaches to boundary and power issues allows for maximum flexibility in both family communication and therapeutic input.

Stage 3 Therapy: What are the Personality Styles, Temperaments, and Interpersonal Polarities in the Family?

☐ Bernice and Fred (Polarity: indulgence versus restrictiveness)

A simple issue such as picking up a child's forgotten doll from the babysitter can lead to a polarized confrontation regarding core personality issues.

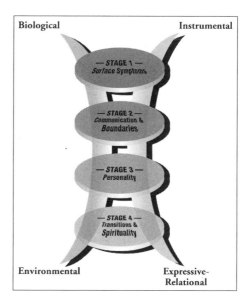

Bernice and Fred originally came to therapy regarding parenting issues. Fred thought that Bernice was too lenient with their 7-year-old daughter, Angela, and Bernice felt that Fred was too strict. Stage 2 work included developing better talking and listening skills and learning how to manage anger. Medications were made available (but not used) to help avoid near-physical disagreements. In a recent session, stage 3 core personality issues were addressed directly.

When Fred picked Angela up from the babysitter, the little girl forgot to bring home her dolly. The family was going on vacation and Angela did not want to go without it. Bernice wanted to go back and get the doll before they left, but Fred was unwilling to make the effort. This led to a major argument that seemed out of proportion to the problem, indicating lifelong issues. Fred felt controlled by Angela's childish forgetting and irrationality, which triggered (with some probing) a scene where Fred felt controlled by his irrational, domineering father, who wanted Fred to clean his military boots. Bernice, in an opposite way, was reminded of how her domineering mother forbade her go to parties or "play." For Fred, getting the dolly felt like irrational submission to the daughter and wife. For Bernice, not getting the dolly meant that her own "7-year-old self" would reexperience the excessive restriction and deprivation that she recalled in her own childhood.

Bernice and Fred illustrate how core personality beliefs and attitudes can distort day-to-day life events. Couples therapy offered Bernice and Fred the chance to see how Fred's fear of domination resulted in overcontrol and how Bernice's fear of deprivation and restriction resulted in her being indulgent. Bernice and Fred were also able to appreciate that the escalating, intense feelings they were experiencing toward each other were distorted by attitudes that, although logical historically, were overreactive in the present.

The therapy consisted of numerous conversations where each spouse listened to the background story of the other. The pros and cons of Fred's restrictiveness and Bernice's indulgence were discussed openly, promoting a middle ground for both. The awareness and expression of Bernice's and Fred's overreaction to a dolly and each other led to greater flexibility in Fred's sense of reacting to being controlled and Bernice's pressure to promote pleasure.

Both Bernice and Fred were very sensitive and had a tendency toward action and aggression. These temperaments and the possible use of medications for anger management were considered in couples therapy, but medications were not used.

Bernice and Fred's case helps illustrate three main clinical issues that must be integrated when the family is ready to address personality-related blocks to communication and problem-solving:

- current family or couple conflicts based on opposing personality characteristics;
- long-term interpersonal attitudes that have become rigid;
- biological temperament vulnerabilities, both genetic and environmental.

As with Bernice and Fred, my preference, in general, is to first clarify and mediate the interpersonal family conflicts based on opposing personality characteristics. As these are clarified, the long-term personality attitudes for each family member (especially the parents or treatment couple) become apparent. Meanwhile, temperament issues regarding thinking, dysphoric mood, anger, and anxiety are evaluated for the appropriate use of pharmacotherapy. Genetic as well as environmentally mediated biological temperament factors can influence the degree of blaming, negativity, aggression, or panic.

After a family deals with surface symptoms and modifies boundary and power issues away from extreme rigidities, personality style problems and conflicts based on personality issues usually come to the foreground. Even when an individual seeks help because of long-term personality and temperament difficulties, rather than immediate symptoms or family organizational issues, I attempt to include other family members or intimate partners in order to observe and experience the interpersonal personality dynamics. Frequently, conflicts are based on opposite personality characteristics (polarities), but partners with similar styles can also experience escalating conflict. Even though core personality issues are often demonstrated in intense reactions between intimate partners, I wait until the therapeutic alliance is sufficiently established before addressing these highly emotional concerns directly.

In stage 1, medication and family therapy can improve family and social interaction by lowering distracting surface symptoms of thinking, mood, violence, and anxiety. In stage 2, medication and therapy should similarly improve communication by enhancing listening and perception. In stage 3, communication is further developed with the help of medication by diversifying stereotypic, rigid, and archaic personality characteristics and styles that block interpersonal conversation and connection.

Personality Styles and Classifications

Each school of psychotherapy describes and classifies personality styles. An understanding of lifelong coping attitudes helps clarify immediate interpersonal conflict. There appear to be three or four major groupings or clusters that, when viewed from different overlapping viewpoints, can help crystallize the long-term character component of the combined personality treatment which also includes biological temperaments and immediate interpersonal grievances. Following is a discussion of several different views of personality and personality disorders.

Personality Classification

**INTERPERSONAL
PERSONALITY DISORDERS**
(Benjamin)

ODD/ECCENTRIC CLUSTER
Paranoid
Schizoid

ANXIOUS/FEARFUL CLUSTER
Dependent
Obsessive-compulsive
Negativistic (passive-aggressive)
Avoidant

DRAMATIC/ERRATIC CLUSTER
Borderline
Narcissistic
Histrionic
Antisocial

MYERS BRIGGS TYPE INDICATOR
(Janowsky)
Extroversion versus introversion
Sensing versus intuition
Thinking versus feeling
Judging versus perceiving

GESTALT CHARACTER "RESISTANCES"
Introjection
Projection
Retroflection
Deflection
Confluence

SATIR PERSONALITY STYLES
Blamer
Placator
Distractor
Rationalizer

FIGURE 5.1.

Interpersonal Personality Disorders (Benjamin, 1993)

One especially relevant classification for the dimensional and interpersonal concepts presented here is the work of Lorna Benjamin (1993). As shown in Figure 5.1, Benjamin outlines the interpersonal dynamics of each personality category within three major categories or clusters: the odd/eccentric group, the dramatic/erratic group, and the anxious/fearful group. Benjamin has taken 10 diagnostic categories from the *Diagnostic & Statistical Manual* (DSM) (1994) and emphasized their interpersonal implications.

In the odd/eccentric group, for example, the "paranoid" interpersonal style is characterized by "a fear that others will attack to hurt, or blame ... The baseline position is to wall off, stay separate, and tightly control the self."

In the dramatic/erratic group, the "borderline" interpersonal style is "a morbid fear of abandonment and a wish for protective nurturance, preferably received by a constant physical proximity to the rescuer. The baseline position is friendly dependency on a nurturer, which becomes hostile control if the caregiver or lover fails to deliver enough." In this same dramatic/erratic group, the "narcissistic" personality style is characterized as having "an extreme vulnerability to criticism or being ignored, together with a strong wish for love, support, and admiring deference from others ... The baseline position involves noncontingent love of self and presumptive control of others."

In the anxious/fearful group, the "obsessive-compulsive" interpersonal style is described as having "a fear of making a mistake or being accused of being imperfect. The quest for order yields a baseline interpersonal position of blaming and inconsiderate control of others. The obsessive-compulsive personality control alternates with blind obedience to authority or principle. There is excessive self-discipline, as well as restraint of feelings, harsh self-criticism, and neglect of the self."

Myers Briggs Type Indicator (Janowsky, 1999b)

Another relevant personality classification system is the Myers Briggs Type Indicator (see Janowsky, 1999b). This Jungian-based scale includes four major dimensions of personality:

1. extroversion versus introversion
2. sensing versus intuition
3. thinking versus feeling
4. judging versus perceiving.

Extroverts prefer people and things to ideas; sensing people prefer facts to possibilities; thinking types prefer impersonal analysis to values; judging types prefer a plan to spontaneity. Each opposite personality type—introvert, intuitive, feeling, perceiving—has the opposite preference.

In family therapy, dialogues are used to illuminate differences and tensions between family members along these dimensions. The therapeutic goal is to create increased flexibility for each family member. The ideal therapist (see Chapter 7) would have a broad enough range to mediate polar personality types along each dimension.

Gestalt Character Resistances and Satir Personality Styles

Gestalt theory lists five main character resistances: introjection, projection, retroflection, deflection, and confluence. Virginia Satir (Satir & Baldwin, 1983) has formulated perhaps the simplest and clearest description of personality styles by dividing them into four groups: the blamer, the placator, the distracter, and the rationalizer. The main therapy goal for personality treatment is to create a greater flexibility so that the individual is not trapped in one rigid perception of the world (see Polster (1995), *A Population of Selves*). Marsha Linehan (1993) uses a similar dialectical model that is especially relevant for correcting the dichotomization or "splitting" of the borderline personality.

☐ Instrumental Versus Expressive-Relational Methods and Psychopharmacology in Stage 3

Having described long-term personality styles and personality interactions, treatment methods will now be discussed. As with each of the previous stages of family therapy, the approaches to helping families and individuals with personality rigidities can be seen along the dimension of instrumental versus expressive-relational. The expressive-relational interpersonal therapies tend to clarify and accentuate the interaction of different styles in the family in order to promote awareness. Using the "paradoxical theory of change" concept, such awareness should by itself lead to improved communication and enhanced flexibility between family members. It is assumed that interpersonal problems and life events can be more effectively faced with less personality rigidity.

Instrumental approaches create experiments where family members reverse roles or "try on" new personality styles. Childhood stories that capture the essence of the personality interactional style can be relived through psychodrama with new "restorative" endings considered. Interestingly, directed dialogues to improve communication regarding personality style differences can be conducted either in an instrumental manner where deficits are corrected, or in an expressive-relational manner where improved connection and interpersonal contact can lead to spontaneous, experiential change in each person.

Joe and Mary (Polarity: fun-loving/superficial versus serious/empathic)

The following marital therapy example illustrates a couple that reached stage 3 of therapy, and where complementary styles led to mutual emotional healing and growth. An environmental, expressive–relational approach was emphasized, without medication.

Joe and Mary came for therapy trying to reconcile after a marital separation. Each in their second marriage, they had numerous grievances about money, control, and commitment. Over a period of 2 years, the couple progressed through three stages of therapy. In a series of stage 1 mediation sessions, the practical problems were negotiated as being distinguishable from underlying personality conflicts and differences.

During stage 2 of therapy, the communication between the couple was enhanced. Mary tended to speak in abstract, global terms; her communication difficulty was the focus of several sessions. She was asked to give clear visual examples and evidence of her concern and to suggest alternatives. Joe also had difficulty simply talking and facing conflicts, since he was uncomfortable with negativity and working beyond the romantic chemistry that he valued in the relationship.

The personality issues and complementary personality conflicts were discussed in Stage 3 of therapy. Joe described growing up with a paranoid mother and a sense of insecurity and unpredictability. After his parents' divorce, he felt insecure and unconnected to his stepmother, and he suppressed his anger and frustrations through school academic performance and sports. He eventually learned better coping skills but openly acknowledged having to suppress emotions in general, and anger in particular. Mary grew up in a wealthy suburb of Chicago and had an upper-class background with high standards and expectations for achievements. She felt that whatever she did was not good enough and that she was unfavorably compared to her brother. Mary felt that the romantic aspect was missing in her first marriage.

During therapy, Mary began to appreciate Joe's fun-loving, spontaneous, gregarious qualities. She could see that she lacked these qualities herself, and that Joe gave her an opportunity to develop this side of her personality. Mary could enjoy the feeling of being a "popular high school girl." Similarly,

Joe began to appreciate the stability and comfort of living with a responsible, empathic person, an experience that had been missing in his upbringing. In this context, Joe could gradually begin to express inner feelings and feel a sense of increasing trust and commitment.

Unfortunately, each side of the complementarity had a negative slant. Joe felt controlled and criticized by Mary, and Mary felt that Joe's secretiveness about inner emotions and his superficial gregariousness all pointed to a lack of commitment and untrustworthiness. In the sessions, their reactions to each other felt like full-blown transferential reactions; the here-and-now circumstances and intense reactions were traced back with Joe and Mary as representations of lifelong stories.

The therapy for this couple was basically expressive-relational; the couple was focused mainly toward clarifying their dynamics and becoming aware of the "sunshine" and "toxic" versions of their personalities. There was also an educational component, as the couple was challenged to own the qualities of the other person that they admired and to develop these qualities internally through experiments of reversing roles. Medication was not used.

Joe and Mary are currently addressing stage 4 issues regarding planning their future and finding meaning in their lives. This topic will be discussed in the next chapter. From time to time, the couple discusses practical issues reminiscent of stage 1 or deals with communication blocks reminiscent of stage 2. Most of the sessions were conjoint, but Joe and Mary each had several individual sessions to more fully discuss their negative and ambivalent thoughts about the other without undue damage. The parents and siblings of each spouse have been invited to participate in therapy but have not, as yet, been able to attend.

Although I had intuitive experiential reactions to Joe and Mary as individuals similar to that of the spouse, my reactions were primarily used to promote and accentuate the interaction between the couple. On occasion, however, Joe would think of me as too controlling and critical, and Mary would think of me as excessively humorous or cavalier. These perceptions of me were clarified and acknowledgment given from my point of view. Subsequently, the reactions toward me were redirected back to the marital work. In short, the emphasis was on transferential distortions between Joe and Mary, rather than on transferential issues with me.

If medications to increase temperament flexibility were to be considered for Joe and Mary, one might consider Joe as having anger and anxiety vulnerabilities that could be helped with a serotonin-enhancing drug (perhaps low doses of Zoloft), a beta blocker such as Inderal, or low doses of an impulse-control medication like Depakote. Mary had a depressive mood vulnerability that might have been treated with an antidepressant (perhaps Prozac or Wellbutrin).

Dwight and Dixie (Polarity: orderly/meticulous versus exuberant/deprived)

In contrast to the previous couple, Dwight and Dixie used psychopharmacology to help negotiate complementary styles. The instrumental versus expressive-relational dichotomy in the couple was reflected in their perception and discussion of the antidepressant used.

Dwight and Dixie, both in their second marriage with Dwight in his 70's and Dixie in her 60's, sought treatment because of excessive bickering. After mediation of numerous fights regarding in-laws, money, sex, and territoriality in their small house, the personality issues of each member of the couple became clear and their tensions around the complementarity of these personalities became the focus of the therapy.

Dixie had always felt deprived and mistreated. This deprivation was especially experienced when she was sent to boarding school for a dyslexic condition. Dixie had felt mistreated in her job, by her former husband, and more recently by her son. She felt deprived by her husband, because he had recently become less sexual and less loving in general.

Dwight described growing up in difficult circumstances. He adapted to his parents' medical problems and alcoholism by becoming orderly and meticulous in his schoolwork and eventually in his career. Despite this orderly demeanor, he was able to be a successful, expressive artist. His main vocation as a quality control inspector for a large company reflected his meticulous style.

Dwight appreciated Dixie's warmth and exuberance and enjoyed going to the theater and having dinner parties and social connections. Dixie tended to organize these parties as well as romantic nightly dinners. Dixie appreciated Dwight's stability and predictability, especially in contrast with the unreliability and infidelity of her first husband.

The couple was helped to understand the limitations of the marriage, and their idealization was made less central to the happiness of each. Dixie, especially, was urged to seek appropriate affirmations and support outside of the marriage. For a period of time, this included a weekly psychotherapy group with me. In addition, Dixie began volunteering at the local hospital and developed a circle of friends that provided gratification for her.

Zoloft was included in Dixie's treatment regimen as an adjunct. Dixie's own perception was that at times her feelings of deprivation and neglect were so deep that she would become irritable and argumentative beyond an acceptable level. The Zoloft controlled this irritability to a remarkable degree, according to both Dwight and Dixie. An open discussion about the potential misuse of medication to "silence the wife" versus the appropriate use to facilitate discussions and communication took place. The latter was the case here. Dwight considered medication a practical way to deal with Dixie's irritability and complaining. Dixie described medication as helping her be more social and preventing her moods from ruining her good time.

Dwight was given directed exercises on being more sympathetic and loving to his wife, since these external demonstrations of love were important
to Dixie. Dixie was given directed exercises to honor Dwight's need for a
schedule and spatial privacy within his environment.

With this strengthened interpersonal personality support system, the
couple is now facing a life crisis: Dixie has been diagnosed with a non-
malignant tumor that nonetheless may threaten her life. The couple is
weighing medical versus surgical alternatives. In addition, Dwight's hearing and memory are gradually deteriorating, leading to more difficulty in
day-to-day communication. These issues reflect stage 4 therapy.

When the Zoloft medication was introduced to the couple, the husband perceived the medication from a functional, instrumental point of
view. His view was that the medication kept the wife's target symptoms
of irritability and depression in check. The wife perceived the medication
from an expressive-relational point of view, since she felt she could actually communicate her complaints and wishes more effectively in the right
context with the help of the medication. The medication gave her the energy and ability to socialize and be more connected with her friends. The
therapist's position was to honor both perceptions of the medication as being valid. The discussion of the medication had therapeutic value beyond
the actual biological effect.

Psychopharmacology can be seen as a medical model—an instrumental
adjunct—to personality treatment, since biological temperaments are actively modified with medication. From a more expressive-relational point
of view, however, medication helps minimize temperament style vulnerabilities and increase flexibility. Communication is enhanced, since a real-
life, current problem is addressed directly rather than with approaches
that may be more appropriate for historical events.

The instrumental use of psychopharmacology is more prevalent in
stage 1, when biological factors are more clearly causing symptoms. Stage 3
personality work, with a more modest use of medication, involves a
more complex mixture of biological temperament factors, developmental trauma, and family dynamics that can distort styles of approaching
life's problems.

For example, if one family member has a personality approach to the
world summarized as "No" and another family member has an approach of
"Yes," any family dispute will predictably end up in a "Yes-No" argument.
In therapy this yes-no interaction can be accentuated, without content, by
having family members simply repeat yes or no, perhaps using different
voice tones. The yes or no confining attitudes interfere with any resolution
of current problems or issues. The yes attitude can be based on mellow or
easy-going biological temperament factors, or it can be based on family or
gender submissiveness experience. Similarly, the no attitude can be based

on biological oversensitivity or on a need to resist dominating forces in the family or culture. The family should be included in an open discussion of biological factors versus environmental factors as causes for current character concerns, as well as a discussion of whether or not medication should be considered.

Money, sex, parenting, and in-laws are the traditional family therapy surface issues in stage 1, and they also reveal stage 3 personality style preferences for addressing life's problems. Family members' personality styles are also revealed when they respond to the idea of medication. The therapist can avoid unnecessary resistance to medication as well as develop a fuller appreciation of personality issues by paying close attention to the attitudes regarding medication.

☐ Understanding Attitudes Toward Pharmacotherapy

In each of Benjamin's (1993) interpersonal personal styles, there is an anticipated "transference" (distorted anachronistic attitude) toward pharmacology. Just as one can understand unrealistic attitudes or metaphors regarding food, sex, or money, an understanding of distortions regarding medications can help the therapist and family consider reluctance/resistance when pharmacotherapy is indicated.

Odd/Eccentric Cluster

Paranoid: The patient might be very concerned about side effects that may be discovered over the next decade. She might point out the drug company's profit motivation. After taking the drug she might feel controlled and unnatural and may consider making a formal complaint.

Schizoid: The patient would be unlikely to consider medications, since there is no expectation that medications would help or that help is needed.

Anxious/Fearful Cluster

Dependent: The patient might tolerate extreme side effects without reporting them for fear of losing the nurturing and caring that the medication represents.

Obsessive-Compulsive: The patient might delay before taking medication, saying that she can control the symptoms. She might consider a medication after extensive Internet research, but then alternate between thinking the medication is a wonderful "magic pill" and thinking it is "useless."

Negativistic (Passive-Aggressive): The patient might reluctantly agree to medication as a last hope but be suspicious of side effects. She might take the wrong dosage and complain about results. The patient might try a series of medications with none "working."

Avoidant: The patient might avoid medication for fear of complications or having the medication indicate that there was "something profoundly wrong" with her. The patient might overdose rather than deal with problems of medication.

Dramatic/Erratic Cluster

Borderline: The patient will probably consider the medication wrong or not enough. It is also likely that the patient will underdose or overdose with the medication.

Narcissistic: This patient might think that her depression is special and that an exotic medication is needed. She may expect free samples and think that her side effects are especially interesting. The patient may become angry if medication does not work and perhaps consider a lawsuit.

Histrionic: This patient typically jokes about being a medication poster child, but gives vague descriptions of symptoms, symptom relief, or side effects. She mentions telling friends about her psychiatrist's special medication cocktails.

Antisocial: This patient might impulsively use medication to get "high" or as a manipulation to apply for disability. The patient might forge prescriptions or sell drugs for profit, without remorse.

In order to encourage optimal use of pharmacotherapy, the therapist should encourage dialogues *within* the family between the instrumental spokespersons and the expressive-relational spokespersons, in addition to discussion with the therapist. This dialogue helps decide about medications, although the recipient of medication would have veto power over any decision. Ira Glick (Glick & Thase, 1997) points out that one advantage of combining psychopharmacology with family treatment is that the family can be a resource in understanding and working through reluctance to taking medication. In addition, education regarding the use of psychopharmacology for problematic but nondiagnosable ("subclinical") temperament styles and personality vulnerabilities can enhance family personality therapy work. Similar instrumental versus expressive-relational dialogues between professionals can also help integrate modern biological therapies with more traditional interpersonal personality therapies.

☐ Biological Versus Environmental Causes and Psychopharmacology in Stage 3

The previous section discussed the importance of understanding the instrumental versus expressive-relational personality dimension in order to create a therapeutic alliance. This section will review the nature versus nurture dimension as related to interpersonal personality therapy. Over the last several years, there has been an explosion of information and research regarding biological factors and emotional difficulties. In Chapter 3, some of the psychological disorders that are more clearly medical or biological were outlined. These disorders include Alzheimer's disease, schizophrenia, manic depressive illness, severe obsessive-compulsive disease, attention deficit and hyperactivity disorders, severe depressions, and certain anxiety disorders and shyness. Pharmaceutical companies have been especially interested in symptoms that appear predominantly organic, where the efficacy of medications can be most easily tested.

   In the arena of personality functioning the situation is much more complex, and biological factors and environmental factors are usually more intermingled. In addition, biological factors include both genetic vulnerabilities, as well as biological changes that are induced by trauma, such as in posttraumatic stress syndromes (see Gunderson & Sabo, 1993). Adding to treatment complexity is the question of the proper mix of individual therapy with interpersonal and family therapy. The author's bias is for using interpersonal and family resources for treating individuals with personality rigidities or symptoms.

☐ Biological Temperament Dimensions

Psychopharmacology can be used in personality work to modify "subclinical" temperaments that are on a continuum with more severe, more clearly biological pathological temperaments and symptoms. Medication is just a small piece of the complex array of treatments needed for rigid personality problems. Robert Cloninger and Larry Siever are both psychiatrists who consider personality difficulties in a continuum of biological versus environmental factors, supporting the integrative power of dimensional thinking.

The Cloninger Model of Personality

Robert Cloninger (Cloninger, Svrakic, & Pryzbeck, 1993; Cloninger & Svrakic, 1997; Cloninger, 1998) tries to distinguish personality factors based on biology (temperament) from personality factors based on training and environmental experience (character). His biological temperament categories include:

* *Novelty seekers*, who look for quick answers to problems by action and changes;
* *Harm avoiders*, who are characterized by negative avoidant reactions to difficulties;
* *Approval seekers*, who depend on outside reinforcement, rewards, and approval from others;
* *Persisters*, who are able to persevere and continue to struggle despite difficulties and fatigue.

Cloninger also identifies three separate environmental categories that are influenced primarily by family and social influences:

* the ability to *accept responsibility*, in contrast to blaming other people or externals for difficulties;
* the ability to be involved in *reciprocal relationships* and cooperation;
* the ability to *look beyond oneself* and have charitable pursuits.

Cloninger's distinction of biological and psychosocial personality factors helps integrate biological approaches for temperament difficulties with psychological and family training for character difficulties.

Thad's Family (Polarity: "nice guy" versus domineering)

In the following clinical example, the family had progressed through stages 1 and 2 of family work. Several years later, Thad came in for personality and life stress issues regarding his "nice-guy" style; he was also concerned about his negative outlook on life. Using the Cloninger model, Thad might have biological temperament issues based on his approval-seeking and harm-avoidance (depression); Thad's sense of charity and good deeds toward others could be considered learned character qualities. Medication was used to facilitate therapy and to modify temperament factors, even though there was no clear diagnosable condition. The main approach was expressive-relational as the patient began to explore his personality in contrast with other family members.

> I have worked with Thad's family for over 18 years. The family first came to me when Thad's younger brother, Evan, then 12, was having difficulties socially and was displaying nervousness despite getting straight A's in school. Eventually, it became clear that his temperament was that of a serious, somewhat obsessive-compulsive perfectionist. His brother Thad was

laid-back and made average grades, but was much more socially involved than Evan. Thad's temperament was in a depressive-moody direction. The father, Jim, was a successful retailer with a blunt, direct, aggressive style. The mother, Mary, a teacher, was somewhat insecure but was very orderly and precise. Over the years, the family was first seen for Evan's nervous agitation (treated with individual and family therapy combined), then for help in mediating teenage conflicts between the two brothers, followed by couples therapy for a marital crisis as a financial recession hit the area, and then a midlife crisis with individual treatment for the mother, who was considering going back to work.

Most recently, Thad, now 32, the sensitive social brother, sought individual therapy for personality issues regarding his "too nice" style. Thad has sought a career helping the homeless and is involved with a woman who he considers compassionate and understanding in situation after situation. Thad describes core insecurities and struggles as the good guy who is sensitive and warm but feels somewhat victimized by previous girlfriends, his coworkers, and his brother Evan, now a stockbroker.

On a recent vacation, Thad and his brother got into an argument because Evan insisted on skiing rules and propriety. Thad felt offended by Evan's authoritarian attack and control and responded rebelliously (more aggressively than he had for years), saying that he was not going to be bossed around by his brother. Thad expressed himself more openly than usual at the time; the serious, critical Evan withdrew, but in retrospect, continued to ruminate about the argument. Thad, in the meantime, satisfied that the issue had been resolved, was able to enjoy the vacation. Because of my understanding of the family relationships and personality opposites, I have been able to more fully understand this kind of interaction and the current round of individual personality therapy with Thad.

Thad has used Wellbutrin to help him deal with the discouragement of this struggle, and this medication has helped facilitate his personality therapy.

One instrumental cognitive method used with Thad included his reexperiencing childhood scenes where he felt humiliated, while being teased for stuttering and scenes that illuminated his relationship with his father. From an adult perspective he "redecided" (redecision therapy of Goulding, 1997) how he could cope. Changes included confronting others (just the way he confronted Evan) rather than himself. In addition, Thad experimented with imaginary dialogues between the submissive and assertive sides of his personality in order to facilitate personality integration (*A Population of Selves*, Polster, 1995).

Thad primarily saw himself as the good guy who finishes last. Evan and the father represented opposite styles of people who are forceful, strategic, and willing to direct and use people. Thad's personality was seen as ranging from the passively controlled good-guy victim all the way to the directive, controlling, healthy narcissistic side. It was clear that the narcissistic side of his personality was not well represented. In therapy, the good guy and the directive sides of the personality were each considered from both a "sunshine" and a "toxic" point of view, similar to object-relations methods (Scharff & Scharff, 1991). The sunshine version of being sensitive and connected was that Thad had many friends and felt a sense of caring for the less fortunate. The positive version of being strategic and directive was being able to get what you want, being successful, and feeling a sense of pride. The toxic version of being a good guy was that people take advantage and that there is occasionally a profound feeling of depression and overwhelming hopelessness, as well as a sense of injustice because goodness and good deeds are not recognized or rewarded. The negative version of the directive side was that Thad was afraid he would be too impersonal, exploitative, and cruel. He was afraid that he would be so strategic that he would lose a sense of humanity and love.

Thad was able to practice exercising the minority (assertive) side of his personality in the imaginary dialogues conducted in the session. Thad became more able to have real dialogues with his brother, with adversaries at work, and with his father, who tended to still tease him. The Wellbutrin was seen as an adjunct to the therapy, not the crucial factor. Its effect was to aid Thad's positive attitude toward therapeutic change and possibilities. Gradually, Thad has felt more balanced and has been more assertive and directive, although he still feels more comfortable with his sensitive and caring side. His current romantic relationship will likely lead to marriage, and he has chosen a person who is similar to himself in terms of caring and generosity compared to a previous girlfriend, who continually berated Thad for not meeting her needs.

Thad's case again illustrates dimensional thinking to bridge:

1. the appropriate stage of personality work;
2. the biological temperament factors (depressive and approval seeking) versus learned character qualites (charity and community service);
3. polarized personalities in the family and social network (passive/sub-missive versus active/domineering);
4. the use of instrumental techniques, in addition to more expressive-relational therapy conversations.

Betsy (Polarity: "bossy"/provocative versus cooperative/friendly)

In contrast to the predominantly environmental/expressive-relational approach used with Thad, this next clinical case illustrates a biological/instrumental approach in working with a 7-year-old's personality and interpersonal style.

Betsy came to the office with her parents. The mother described her as having a difficult temperament ever since she was born. The mother had been reading about bipolar personality problems and became aware that the daughter had been difficult in terms of moodiness, irritability, and social aggression for as long as she could remember. The mother wondered whether there was some medication to help with what she considered an organic situation.

At first, I was concerned that the daughter was a projection of the mother's needs and a scapegoat for the family and marital difficulties; on the other hand, Betsy did have many of the features that I associated with a bipolar temperament. She was effervescent, unusually seductive for a 7-year-old, and extremely provocative and moody. The school reported her as being bossy, antagonistic, and hostile to the other children.

I decided to introduce low doses of Prozac (10 mg/day) for anxiety and depression combined with low doses of Lithium (300 mg/day) for the bipolar (cyclothymic) temperament. Within a few weeks, Betsy seemed to miraculously change and was no longer an obstreperous, difficult youngster. (The use of Prozac needed to be monitored carefully because of the risk of inducing mania.) After a time, Betsy became popular with her peers, more sensitive to others, and was elected a class officer. The school reported a major change in likability and affect, and this change lasted for a year of medication and intermittent family plus individual psychotherapy.

At that point, the parents decided to discontinue the medication since things were going so well. During the 2-month period when Betsy was off medication, the previous negative interactions returned, and the parents found their daughter extremely difficult. Medications have been resumed with a return to the likable, connected, "popular self." Although it is hoped that through therapy and family meetings the patterning and self-esteem can be solidified internally without medication, it is clear that this child has benefited from normal social development and improved school involvement, even though her personality improvement still appears dependent on the medication rather than being a true, behavioral, generalized change.

One important topic raised by this clinical example is the duration of therapy. The author's practice is to have a flexible range from very short-term therapy (if changes and desired goals are reached and the family prefers, for financial or other reasons, to limit the scope of the therapy) to longer therapy (especially for complex developmental and traumatic situations). The use of psychopharmacology, when effective, speeds the process of therapy.

Siever Temperament Spectrums

Larry Siever (Siever & Davis, 1991; Siever, New, Kirrane, Novotny, Koenigsberg, & Grossman, 1998) also presents a useful model of

TEMPERAMENT DIMENSIONS (Siever)

Thinking:	Schizoid style and vulnerability versus schizophrenia and paranoia *(Zyprexa, Risperdal, Seroquel, Haldol, Clozaril, Mellaril)*
Dysphoric Mood:	Self-blaming, irritable, negative style and vulnerability versus depression and depressive paranoia *(Prozac, Zoloft, Paxil, Celexa, Serzone, Wellbutrin SR, Effexor SR)*
Violence/Anger:	Impulsive, action-oriented, irritable style and vulnerability versus mania, violence and paranoia *(Depakote, Topamax, Lithium, Inderal, Risperdal, Zyprexa, Haldol, Mellaril, SSRIs)*
Anxiety/Stress:	Sensitivity to stimuli or change style and vulnerability versus panic, phobia and paranoia *(SSRIs, Serzone, Xanax, Klonopin, Inderal, Lithium, Depakote, Neurontin, Risperdal)*

FIGURE 5.2.

biological contributions to personality and temperament functioning and, in addition, outlines a spectrum from less severe personality and temperament vulnerabilities to overt severe target symptoms (see Figure 5.2). Severe symptoms, early onset, and a strong family history are at the end of the continuum that shows more biological pathology. By noting which categories of medications are most effective for which personality factors, Siever indicates four crucial biological factors in personality. These four factors are modern versions of the original Greek neurohumors. They include difficulties in thinking, mood regulation, violence and temper management, and anxiety/stress management.

Thinking Continuum

In the *thinking* arena, the "atypical" antipsychotics (newer, mixed, biochemical-altering medications with lower muscular side effects) have been especially useful in controlling schizophrenic symptoms and psychotic thinking. These medications include Zyprexa, Risperdal, Seroquel, and Clozaril. Clozaril has been perhaps the drug of choice in terms of efficacy, but because one side effect is dangerously lowering the white blood cell count (making a person vulnerable to infection), this drug has not been widely used. Seroquel is a more recent addition for treating psychotic thinking; newer atypical medications such as Zeldox (with less weight gain) are also expected to be effective. Zyprexa has been useful for bipolar and schizophrenic psychosis but has the side effects of weight gain and drowsiness. There is also some concern that Zyprexa may alter glucose metabolism, causing diabetes. Risperdal is currently the most popular antipsychotic, but it can occasionally cause muscular twitching or restlessness. Resperdal is especially effective for treating the cognitive impairment of schizophrenia, i.e., recent memory and "executive thinking." Seroquel does not have muscular side effects but can cause drowsiness.

Knowing that these medications can be useful for symptoms of the severe thinking disorders described in Chapter 3, Siever points out a continuum that includes individuals who appear to have a mild schizoid style characterized by a low level of paranoia and a lack of expressive speech. The basic idea is that the same medication, usually in lower doses, is useful at this end of the continuum where there is no diagnosable condition, but only a "style." In this "subclinical" or "subsyndromal" personality style, one can see the elements of diminished affect, a lack of sociability, and individualized, somewhat peculiar or bizarre thought processes. The concept is that low doses of medication would help schizoid individuals be more connected and more communicative.

A definition of healthy personality functioning is the ability to experience the world in a flexible, multidimensional way, which permits interpersonal connection, cooperation, and adaptability to change. If the medication is effective, not only would certain thinking and behavioral characteristics be modified, but such modification would result in better communication and connection with other family members and social contacts.

Expanding knowledge about the "thinking continuum," Judith Rapoport (1999a), in her research on childhood schizophrenia at the National Institute of Mental Health, has conceptualized medication as delaying, rather than preventing, the onset of a more full-blown schizophrenic picture. In a 1999 presentation on her recent research findings at the American Psychiatric Association, she jokingly stated that if we could delay a full-blown schizophrenic syndrome until the patient was 90 years old, then the medication would help control the full expression of a biological condition sufficiently without "curing" that condition. Rapoport's findings support the speculation that certain personality styles may be modifiable before they become full-blown personality disorders or result in major symptoms. Obviously, there is an ethical consideration as to whether or not problems should be treated before they are manifested (and whether the soft signs or family history are sufficiently predictive).

Very low doses of Risperdal (for example, 0.25–0.5 mg per day versus a regular dose of 4 mgs per day) can be used when individuals have anxiety or other interpersonal difficulties and a schizoid temperament or family history of schizophrenia. To the extent that low doses of atypical antipsychotics can be used to enhance sociability and connectivity, the medication creates a situation where family influences and psychotherapy can proceed at a more beneficial rate. It is unfortunate that this group of medications has been called "antipsychotic." For clinical purposes, it is more appropriate to call these medications "major tranquilizers"; an even better name might be "temperament enhancers."

Dysphoric Mood Continuum

Siever's continuum of *mood* includes a biological temperament vulnerability characterized by a low level of moodiness, lack of pleasure, and negativity. Siever conceptualizes this vulnerability along a continuum where, under particular stressors or in a cyclical manner, people with this temperament can develop full-blown severe depression. Lewis Judd and colleagues (1996, 1998) at the Department of Psychiatry at the University of California, San Diego have also explored the prevalence of subclinical depression and have found that many people with chronic moodiness, irritability, and unhappiness—about 5% of the population—actually have a low-level biological malady that can be effectively treated with antidepressants and therapy.

Giovanni Fava (Fava et al., 1998), an Italian researcher mentioned in Chapter 1, notes that chronic depression is frequently treated better by behavioral therapies or behavioral methods plus medication, rather than by medication alone. However, he proposes that medication may be better for the initial phase of treating acute symptoms. He states that a combination of medication and therapy works better for the chronically "unhappy" (but nonsymptomatic) phase, with psychotherapy preventing symptomatic relapses at a higher rate than medication. Fava's work also integrates pharmacology and psychological methods for mood problems, including a feeling of unhappiness, which is not diagnosable as depression. As mentioned earlier, although Fava integrates psychological therapy with biological therapy, both are instrumental, corrective therapies.

As with the previous *thinking* dimension, where a schizoid temperament can lead all the way to full-blown schizophrenic symptoms, the continuum of **"mood"** or depression is equally complex. The biological element is considered an important component of the personality picture, but there are also many family, gender, developmental, cultural, educational, and transitional elements of personality to consider.

Again, the use of a particular medication for mood/temperament problems is extrapolated from the more severe end of the continuum. The advent of the serotonin agents, with Prozac being introduced in the late 1980's, has changed the practice of family psychiatry. Four main serotonin-enhancing agents are now on the market.

- *Prozac*, the first selective serotonin reuptake inhibitor (SSRI) has a significant side effect of delayed sexual response. (The same is true of the other three main SSRIs—Zoloft, Paxil, and Celexa.) Prozac also has a long half-life, which means that it takes longer for Prozac to leave the bloodstream in the event of a complication, such as the drug-induced mania that can occur with SSRIs.
- *Zoloft* is sometimes complicated by diarrhea and a withdrawal syndrome characterized by nausea and a feeling of sickness if the medication is stopped abruptly.
- *Paxil*, although creating a higher level of serotonin, is not significantly more effective than other agents. Paxil has anticholinergic properties that can create constipation and dry mouth. Patients frequently gain weight on Paxil.
- *Celexa*, the newest serotonin agent, also causes sexual side effects and drowsiness. One advantage of Celexa is that it interacts less with other medications than the previous three. Prozac, Zoloft, and Paxil inhibit liver enzymes, delaying the metabolism of other coadministered medications.

Serzone is an additional serotonin agent that has fewer sexual side effects compared to the other four. Its main side effect is drowsiness. Wellbutrin heads a separate category of antidepressants. Wellbutrin enhances both the norepinephrine and dopamine systems and is especially popular since it usually does not have sexual side effects. Wellbutrin is basically a stimulant; the introduction of the sustained-release form has reduced the previous problem with seizures as a side effect. John Feighner (1999) describes research on new antidepressants. One is "substance P," a neurokinin related to the platelet serotonin transport system; also on the horizon are the synthetic pentapeptides related to melatonin.

For treating mild mood vulnerability and negative temperament styles, the question is whether lower doses of the same medications can be useful. From the author's experience, results are promising.

Stephen Stahl (2000) has popularized the use of combination psychopharmacology treatments (for mood as well as for thinking, violence, or anxiety disorders), although he has clearly stated his preference for single-drug treatments. Multiple drugs can be an advantage in treatment-resistant situations because varied therapeutic mechanisms are introduced. For example, combining Wellbutrin and Prozac produces the serotonin-enhancing effect of Prozac plus the norepinephrine/dopamine effect of Wellbutrin. In addition, even in low-dose situations for temperament difficulties, the side effects of medications can be used to cancel out each other. For example, the stimulating effects of Wellbutrin could be canceled by the sedating effects of Serzone. Other drugs, such as Effexor, have a dual mechanism of action built in, with a more sedating effect noted in lower doses, and a more stimulating effect noted in higher doses. Effexor in the sustained release form is an excellent dual-action antidepressant, usually used as a back-up medication if the first line antidepressant is ineffective. For personality work, medication addresses the depressive temperament and mood vulnerability, rather than treating a full-blown depression.

Violence and Anger Continuum

The third Siever personality/temperament category is the *violence and anger* continuum. Individuals at the lower level of expression may be irritable, impulsive, and quick to react. At the symptomatic end of the continuum, where the expression of anger is clearly maladaptive, the impulse control problems and violence are extreme. Several medications have become popular for anger management. For temperament and personality issues, as before, these medications are used in lower doses and as a preventative.

Emil Coccaro (1998) has emphasized "irritable depression" as the underlying problem in impulsive aggression. Serotonin-enhancing agents are the preferred treatment for such episodic, unpremeditated violence.

Bipolar manic-depressive illness has also been implicated in aggression. Susan McElroy (1999) has postulated that as many as 50% of the violent outbursts that present to the emergency room may have a bipolar component; she recommends that medications used for manic depressive illness, especially Depakote (or Zyprexa), be used for violence.

There appears to be a spectrum of a bipolar temperament (cyclothymic temperament) from vulnerability to diagnosable conditions. The continuum ranges from a low level of elation to a Bipolar II condition (with depression and intermittent frequent periods of moderate elation, exuberance, sleeplessness, hypersexuality, and grandiosity that are less than a full-blown manic episode), or from a low level of elation to a Bipolar I condition (with full-blown but less frequent manic episodes mixed with depression). The cyclothymic temperament includes industriousness, flamboyance, attractiveness, preoccupation with sexuality, racing thoughts, and generosity; although appealing, people with this temperament frequently have problems with intimacy and depression intermingled (see Akiskal & Akiskal, 1992; Akiskal, 1996; Perugi, Akiskal, Ramacciotti, Naccini, Toni, Milanfranchi, & Musetti, 1999). If the cyclothymic temperament contributes to clinical difficulties, Akiskal recommends low doses of Lithium (for example, 600 mgs per day) combined with low doses of Depakote (for example, 500 mgs per day). This combination balances Lithium's side effect of mental confusion and Depakote's side effects of weight gain and drowsiness.

Kay Jamison (1995) points out that many creative geniuses had a bipolar temperament, although frequently accompanied by symptomatic depression or mania. Her list includes poet Walt Whitman, painters Paul Gauguin, Vincent Van Gogh, and Georgia O'Keefe, composer Gustaf Mahler, songwriter Cole Porter, authors Virginia Wolf, Sylvia Plath, Herman Hesse, and Ernest Hemingway, playwright Tennessee Williams, and musician Charles Mingus. It is thought that the bipolar temperament in these artists contributed to their creativity; the clinical challenge is to help when interpersonal difficulties develop.

Medications that are especially useful for bipolar aggression are also useful for aggression from any cause. These medications are Depakote and Lithium, either individually or sometimes in combination; they are sometimes referred to as "mood stabilizers." In addition, the atypical antipsychotics, Risperdal and Zyprexa, have been used for anger management, with the older antipsychotics such as Mellaril or Haldol occasionally used for acute anger management. (There has been a recent drug alert regarding cardiac side effects for Mellaril.) Inderal, a beta-blocker, has also been effective for anger management, and the serotonin-enhancing agents, especially Zoloft and Paxil, can help reduce impulsive anger. Topamax, which is an antiseizure medication like Depakote, has also been introduced for anger management and impulse control. Topamax is a unique anger management/sedative drug in that it also promotes weight loss. As with the antidepressants, the antianger medications are sometimes used in combination in especially difficult situations.

Anxiety/Stress Continuum

The *anxiety/stress* continuum—Siever's fourth and final continuum—is based on the development of drugs that are effective in helping to manage anxiety and stress. Again, the continuum ranges from vulnerability characterized by "sensitivity" to the environment (see Aron, 1996) to severe, immobilizing panic attacks and debilitating phobias. Therapy to help anxieties and fears hinges on an artful combination of exposure therapy and tolerance of the environmental stimulants, combined with protection and avoidance of these same stimulants, if overly arousing. The medications to treat anxiety can be counterproductive if they create a situation where the patient avoids all troublesome environmental factors and never learns to cope with frustration. The ideal use of medication is to help the patient gradually overcome fears and anxieties and to change these excessive fears to appropriate concerns and caution.

The previously popular medications for anxiety, Xanax and Klonopin, can be effective in reducing anxiety symptoms, but they are used less frequently than serotonin agents, because they supress the functioning of the entire brain rather than more localized anxiety centers and, also, because they can be addictive. In addition, if the patient is trying to cope with recent traumatic stress, Xanax or Klonopin interferes with the natural coping memory mechanisms. Serotonin-enhancing agents are the current recommended treatment for anxiety disorders. If the anxiety appears to be combined with a schizoid picture, Risperdal or Zyprexa in low doses is beneficial. If the anxiety includes racing thoughts and an elated mood or hypersexuality (implying a bipolar mood component), then Depakote or Lithium would be preferred, although medications can be considered in combination. Because Inderal can also control anxiety without a loss of mental functioning, it is popular with public speakers, actors, politicians, and lawyers. Neurontin, another anti-seizure medication, appears to be more effective for anxiety than for violence.

There has been much research regarding posttraumatic stress, and the incidence of child abuse is now known to be much greater than previously thought. Although some people are genetically sensitive to trauma, stress in itself can create biological changes. In posttraumatic stress, damage to the hippocampus area of the brain has been observed (McEwen, 1997). This damage would help explain subsequent difficulty in filtering incoming stimuli. In addition, research has demonstrated (see Yehuda, 1998) that the cortisol feedback system can be overly stimulated after a traumatic event, resulting in a paranoia-like chronic sensitivity. Also, it has become clear that children victimized by physical and sexual abuse eventually develop numerous difficulties, including personality disorders.

John Gunderson (Gunderson & Sabo, 1993; Wheelis & Gunderson, 1998) has described the relationship of developmental trauma as well as biological posttraumatic stress to the borderline personality disorder. Again, the need for biological/environmental integration is apparent for treating and preventing personality disturbance. Joseph LeDoux, in his book *The Emotional Brain* (1996), has made a significant contribution by describing how fearful events create a chain of biological reactions in the brain. He points out that one traumatic experience can create a reaction where the brain perceives numerous environmental stimuli, which are paired with the perceived or actual threat, as being life-threatening. LeDoux points out that this conditioned response of the brain and body is preverbal, and that frequently, medications are the best hope for addressing the physiological response to anticipated danger and abuse.

There has been continued interest in understanding childhood temperaments and, as with adults, research to determine the combination of biological, genetic, traumatic, and interpersonal/environmental factors that can lead to clinical difficulties over time (e.g., see Schwartz, Snidman, & Kagan, 1999). One current conceptualization, similar to the categories above, is to consider three clusters of childhood temperaments:

- *Schizoid detached* children, with somewhat bizarre mannerisms, dress, and quality of thought;

- *Dramatic, impulsive, expressive* children, who are frequently difficult to handle;
- *Anxious* children, with difficulty in social interactions, separation sensitivity, and fears.

Interestingly, it is frequently difficult to predict which temperament styles will remain constant throughout a lifetime, although the schizoid temperament appears to be relatively unchanging. Like the model for adults, medications for children are chosen to match the problematic temperament continuum.

Medications have been over-prescribed, frequently without proper follow-up, for children's temperament difficulties. The author proposes a careful, modest use of medications in a family therapy context.

It is important to emphasize once more that medication for personality difficulties should not be presented as the main modality of treatment. Instead, the medication should be very conservatively presented as an adjunct to psychotherapy and family intervention that will create flexibility and interpersonal dialogues. Many authors have described personality issues along the biological versus environmental continuum. The clinician can carefully include medication in stage 3 to increase personality flexibility and to reduce the blocks to intimate personal contact created by personality rigidities. The family is educated as to the complexity of integrating biological, family, cultural, and gender factors in understanding personality functioning and is included in considering personality experiments and medication.

☐ Paths to Personality Therapy

As a family psychiatrist, I have observed two main paths for entering personality therapy. The first one involves the family presenting with a child having a problem. After this problem is addressed, and hopefully modified to a certain extent in stage 1, boundary and other organizational issues are addressed in stage 2. By this time, the personality issues are usually quite clear, and it is in stage 3 that the therapeutic alliance is sufficient to deal with these long-standing personality attitudes and rigidities. In this first path, the personality issues are usually addressed as marital conflicts in stage 3, with the parents each having a transferential reaction toward each other, or toward me, regarding core personality issues and polarities.

The second main path for personality issues typically involves a married or unmarried couple, without children, trying to resolve their differences and perhaps deciding whether to preserve their relationship. Such a couple would go through the same four stages of therapy outlined for families with children. Les Kadis and Ruth McClendon (1995, 1998) have outlined the different schools of marital therapy that parallel the stages of this book: behavioral problem-solving methods, communication methods, personality interactional methods, and spiritual-loving methods. In their own work, Kadis and McClendon combine experiential gestalt family work with transactional analysis (psychodynamic) commentary. Like the current dimensional staging model, Kadis and McClendon integrate problem-solving with understanding related developmental and personality contextual vulnerabilities and reversing three- or four-generational dysfunctional family patterns.

A third avenue for personality work, instead of a child's misbehavior being a "ticket of admission" for therapy, occurs when an individual or a family identifies a temperament or personality difficulty in an individual who comes for help. At this point, I prefer to invite the rest of the family to participate in an evaluation. Occasionally, stage 1 and 2 can be bypassed and personality and temperament factors can be the foreground rather than the background. Especially in stage 3, it should be emphasized that all three or occasionally four generations of the family are invited to participate (see Framo, 1992).

Walt and Amy (Polarity: thinking/compulsive versus feeling/spontaneous)

Walt and Amy followed the path toward marital work after progressing through stages 1 and 2 of family therapy involving children as well as a premarital evaluation. The experiences of those stages built a therapeutic alliance that allowed for marital/personality explorations which were primarily environmental and primarily expressive-relational, although Prozac and Elavil were used at one point. It is not uncommon for a family therapist to see families intermittently over many years for various issues. Such is the case here, as it was for Thad, who was discussed earlier.

> I have been seeing Walt and Amy off and on for 16 years. I initially met Walt as he was going through a divorce from a highly critical, successful professional woman. He was a physicist, who had originally sought an academic match but was considering marrying Amy who, as a secretary, had a lesser station in life. Walt loved Amy's warmth and connectiveness, and his decision to marry was supported in individual and conjoint therapy with Amy.
>
> Over the years there have been different stages of the therapy, including helping with the two children, who have opposite personalities. One child, Mike, had difficulties with oppositionalism and anxiety as he attended school while the other child, Carol, was easy-going, had many friends, and had no apparent psychological difficulties except a conflict with her brother. In the course of discussing parenting issues, the personality issues in the marriage

became more apparent. Conjoint marital sessions without children were begun. Walt's parents were included in the therapy for one session and described Walt as being the good boy, in contrast to his brother.

Walt was a hard-driving workaholic who was extremely well respected in his field. He always took on extra assignments, political positions, and research projects. Even in the sessions he took copious notes. By contrast, Amy had grown up with four brothers and sisters and felt comfortable in interpersonal conflict and communication. She was warm and generous and tended to go along with Walt's style and needs. Eventually, however, she felt frustrated that she was left doing all the work for the children with Walt coming in for overly permissive cameo appearances. She also felt that Walt paid no attention to her needs and feelings and that she was being ignored.

In addition to changes resulting from therapeutic dialogues between marital personality polarities, a major shift occurred through a naturalistic experiment. Walt developed back pain and required surgery for a herniated disc. He was unable to work for a period of months and found himself at home more with his wife and enjoying the break from his compulsive routine. Since that time, Walt has accepted the challenge of making his marriage and his family more of a priority, as well as emphasizing his own relaxation and self-indulgence. Prozac and Elavil (for back pain) seemed to facilitate Walt's trying on his alter ego.

Walt and Amy each described their family histories and backgrounds, occasionally using reenactments that helped them understand their current styles. Walt had a brother who had an opposite style; Walt described himself as the "good boy" who always did the proper work and was churchgoing. The brother had a history of delinquency, school failure, and provocativeness. Walt enacted imaginary dialogues with the brother to accentuate (and integrate) their personality polarities. Walt was now more able to play hooky.

The openly stated therapeutic agenda for Walt and Amy was to have each of them balance his or her own personality by including a complementary quality demonstrated in the partner. Amy began to take a more "selfish" orientation toward her activities and recreation, and Walt became more attentive, empathic, and relaxed. Like many of the other couples discussed, Walt and Amy demonstrate the power of interpersonal dialogues in revealing personality characteristics and modifying them through polarity integration.

The concept of polarity integration in personality therapy parallels a basic theme of this book: challenging professional methods that are polarized and challenging biological versus environmental advocates who are dichotomized, just like two rigid personalities. As with personality integration and flexibility work, the goal professionally is to reduce polarization and dichotomization by bridging the entire dimension. Being aware of the range of the dimension, and the possibility of thinking along the entire dimension, is a cornerstone to the therapeutic process of integration.

Personality Characteristic Polarities

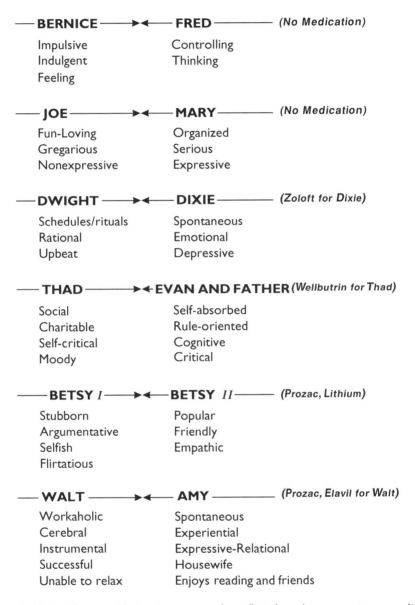

— **BERNICE** ——▶◀—— **FRED** ———— *(No Medication)*

Impulsive	Controlling
Indulgent	Thinking
Feeling	

—— **JOE** ————▶◀—— **MARY** ———— *(No Medication)*

Fun-Loving	Organized
Gregarious	Serious
Nonexpressive	Expressive

—**DWIGHT** ——▶◀— **DIXIE** ———— *(Zoloft for Dixie)*

Schedules/rituals	Spontaneous
Rational	Emotional
Upbeat	Depressive

—— **THAD** ————▶◀**EVAN AND FATHER** *(Wellbutrin for Thad)*

Social	Self-absorbed
Charitable	Rule-oriented
Self-critical	Cognitive
Moody	Critical

—— **BETSY** *I* ——▶◀— **BETSY** *II* ——— *(Prozac, Lithium)*

Stubborn	Popular
Argumentative	Friendly
Selfish	Empathic
Flirtatious	

—— **WALT** ————▶◀—— **AMY** ———— *(Prozac, Elavil for Walt)*

Workaholic	Spontaneous
Cerebral	Experiential
Instrumental	Expressive-Relational
Successful	Housewife
Unable to relax	Enjoys reading and friends

FIGURE 5.3. After considering interpersonal conflicts based on current personality characteristics and polarities, long-term attitudes and styles are considered together with biological temperaments to reduce interpersonal distortions and rigidity.

One contemporary change in family therapy is the immense amount of information available to family clients through books, newspapers, radio, and TV, as well as the Internet. An attempt should be made to educate families regarding the information presented when considering medication or other treatment options.

To summarize the information in this chapter to families, the therapist would emphasize the following:

1. the difference between biological temperament and environmental character;
2. how one can use the treatment of severe conditions to inform prevention or modification of mild conditions;
3. the ability of stress to change the brain and hormonal systems;
4. the range of environmental approaches;
5. the differences between stage 3 personality/interpersonal work and the other stages.

In each of the clinical situations discussed in this chapter, the healing flexibility is promoted by accenting the differences, promoting dialogue and bridging between the polar positions, and understanding the history of each position. Core personality issues become quickly and spontaneously available in interpersonal work, but caution and deliberateness in therapy are crucial to preserve the therapeutic alliance. The examples include psychopharmacology to assist the therapy process and to support the integration of the complementary position, rather than to fix a clearly diagnosable condition. The use of medication over the last decade has increasingly given new support to personality work in general and interpersonal family personality work in particular. As an interesting side note, David Janowsky (1999a) notes that patients on antidepressants or stimulants report, in addition to personality changes, an increased positive response toward their therapy and their therapist. As mentioned in Chapter 2, Wolkowitz (Knutson, Wolkowitz, Cole, Chan, Moore, Johnson, Terpstra, Turner, & Reus, 1998) has conducted similar research demonstrating increased friendliness, a feeling of well-being, and an enhanced positive outlook when Paxil, a serotonin-enhancing agent, was given to normal volunteers without any diagnosable depression. (Also, see Kramer, 1993).

The complexity of personality work with families necessitates a view that includes many modalities and is sensitive to the family's receptivity for intervention. This chapter has attempted to illuminate some of those challenges by incorporating the dimensional bridging approach with clinical examples. Therapy work that integrates personality characteristic polarities as well as core attitude polarities, both interpersonally and individually, can be enhanced by the careful use of psychopharmacology.

Stage 4 Therapy: What are the Family Transitions, Universal Life Challenges, and Spiritual Support Systems?

After a family solves practical problems, improves communication, and reduces rigid personality blocks to intimacy, concerns about universal questions such as the meaning of life and death come into the foreground. Life challenges, limitations, and transitions provide the contextual backdrop for the earlier stages of therapy.

Life-change concerns fall into two main categories: natural evolutionary transitions and traumatic unnatural events. Natural family transitions include aging, graduation, marriage, birth, and death in old age.

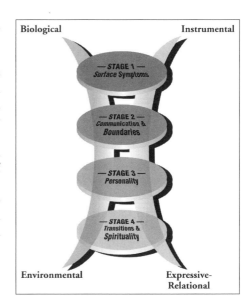

Unnatural traumatic challenges include disasters such as earthquakes and floods, traumatic accidents, murder, suicide, and premature death. In the highest functioning families without significant organizational or personality difficulties, the initial primary concern of family therapy can be the family's developmental transition, coping with the aftermath of a traumatic event, or facing the basic limitations of human existence. More commonly, the therapeutic alliance is developed gradually as the family first faces more concrete practical concerns.

Awareness of spiritual principles is useful at all stages of family therapy, even though such principles are the foreground in stage 4 of therapy, as the family prepares to end formal therapeutic contact. For example, hope and faith are crucial at the beginning of therapy; belonging and membership are important in stage 2; acceptance of personality limitations, reduction of narcissism, and release from overcontrol are crucial for stage 3. In stage 4 the spiritual guidelines are spelled out more directly and applied to universal life problems. The therapist becomes a spiritual guide, but increasingly empathizes with the family about some of the basic questions of life that have no answers. This chapter presents spiritual concepts that are separate and distinct from formal religious scriptures or belief in God.

As an introduction, two clinical examples will be presented. The first involves Rachel, who was discussed in Chapter 4 regarding her tendency to have aloof "high boundaries" while being a "nondirective" follower. Her situation illustrates the practical treatment for a posttraumatic reaction, with a subsequent discussion about death and other spiritual concerns.

> Rachel had completed her therapy and was happily remarried to Tony when the couple returned for help after a fatal auto accident. The couple was travelling with their two sons to the desert when an elderly woman drove her pickup truck from a side street in front of Tony and Rachel's car. Rachel was driving and witnesses confirmed that she was not at fault, and, in fact, did everything she could to avoid the truck. Rachel, Tony, and the two boys were hospitalized for minor injuries, but the driver of the pickup truck was killed instantly.
>
> Rachel developed panic attacks with a feeling of pressure on her chest. She felt slightly "paranoid" and could not watch television news or read the newspaper; she had to leave a movie because of anxiety about death. Tony and the children had no obvious lingering dysfunction although everyone had been very upset.
>
> Tony became a "cotherapist" as he helped conduct a grieving ritual at home. For a 15-minute period each day, Rachel expressed her thoughts and feelings about the accident, the woman she had killed, and the eight or so deaths that she pictured from losses earlier in her life. In a separate 15-minute time period, Tony and Rachel discussed life-affirming topics such as the tenderness and beauty of their sons, the sensual beauty of the sunset, and their love for each other.

Zoloft in doses of 50 mg per day helped with Rachel's fears. Conjoint sessions gave Rachel an opportunity to discuss the untimely deaths of several close friends and her own fear of dying. Rachel also commiserated directly with the deceased woman's family. After the symptoms resolved, in 2 months, the couple began to examine their spiritual beliefs about affirming life in the face of tragedy.

In traumatic situations, the body's cortisone system can occasionally overrespond, resulting in an excessive sensitivity that becomes disabling (see Yehuda, 1998). Fortunately, in Rachel's situation, Zoloft plus therapy and time helped her recover. In the therapy, Rachel's previous coping style of being self-sufficient and stoical was supported, although she was educated as to the value of expressing her memories, anxieties, and fear of death. As briefly mentioned in Chapter 1 in the *Ordinary People* example, the mourning rituals described by Evan Imber-Black (Imber-Black & Roberts, 1992) are extremely valuable for families facing loss. Posttraumatic situations can be conceptualized as coexisting mourning and trauma-recovery periods. The trauma recovery requires a safe haven where the family can merely "survive" the event. Practical arrangements and help are crucial. The mourning process of facing and accepting the loss is emphasized later.

The most recent series of six therapy sessions have recapitulated the four stages of therapy for Rachel and Tony. Initial symptoms were relieved, the couple's connection was reaffirmed, Rachel's need for distance and stoicism were supported but gently challenged, and the couple, after a period of mourning, addressed deeper spiritual concerns about valuing life, especially after being humbled by the near-death experience.

The next clinical example illustrates a life transition that resulted in a new spiritual awareness in the patient. A lifelong coping style of action, exploiting others, and merely surviving, gave way to human intimacy, pursuing a calling that felt useful and productive, and a renewed commitment to fathering. The patient began to accept his previous poverty, childhood neglect, addiction history, and vulnerability to depression, at a deeper level. Previously, these same concerns had been addressed in a more pragmatic and problem-solving manner.

A professional in his 40's, Rick had been seen initially in a family context. The first stage of therapy (surface problems) addressed his wife's complaints that he had a sexual addiction. It became clear over time that the wife was seeking a divorce. In the second stage of therapy, Rick's ability to be intimately loving and empathic with his children was directly observed. However, in his profession and adult interpersonal life most of his relationships had been characterized by his being dominating and exploitative. With his wife and other adults, Rick remained distant with high boundaries; he was instrumental rather than expressive-relational. In stage 3 personality work,

Rick worked through a lifelong depression that was underlying his sexual addiction, which had protected him for many years. Rick had grown up in poverty with a mother who was a prostitute. He dealt with shame issues stemming from a childhood in which he found only glimmers of support and affirmation. With the help of antidepressants and impulse control drugs (Wellbutrin SR and Lithium), Rick has been able to establish an intimate romantic relationship that includes loving sex, instead of compulsive symptomatic sex. With the help of a sexual addictions group, Rick has also been able to control his symptom and he has also become more successful at work.

Arriving at stage 4 of therapy after 2 years, Rick began to consider existential questions about how he wanted to spend his anticipated remaining 40 years. Survival modes and competitive modes had previously characterized his life, and for the first time he appeared to have the energy and interest to directly address philosophical and spiritual issues. There was a continued mild depression as he considered various choices in life including how to best father his children and whether to consider starting a new family. He began to confront the lack of passion he had for his current profession and to yearn for the time when he was a lifeguard and felt important. This life transition and spiritual stage of therapy included readings and philosophical discussions regarding universal questions about life. Rick has decided to continue antidepressants to keep the previous depression and addiction under control, while he addresses deeper philosophical and life questions. The medications helped stabilize Rick so that he could address these higher-level concerns.

As will be outlined below, spiritual concerns were involved at each stage of therapy, not just in the more explicit discussions of stage 4. Hope had been instilled in stage 1, love and connection were encouraged in stage 2, acceptance of human impulses and a release from trying to control the uncontrollable were discussed as personality factors in stage 3.

Most families who seek help do so while they are undertaking life transitions. Dealing with a new marriage, the birth of children, or the emancipation of children leads many families to seek therapy. Traumatic transitions include illness, financial setbacks, and natural disasters or adversity. A basic clinical point is that family discussions can be used to therapeutically debate whether developmental transitions should be intensified or slowed down in order to preserve the status quo. There is a benefit in having a family discuss to what extent the life-change issues are natural, biological, and genetic events and to what extent they are learned environmental or systemic problems that may be more easily changed.

Many developmental changes involve a family's decision to either speed or delay a transition. A typical example would be a child's emancipating from home. The family has to decide whether it is better to prolong the status quo of dependency or whether it is better to promote autonomy. Most families present either because they are trapped in a delayed developmental transition or because a transition has been thrust on the family (in a traumatic manner through death, adversity, or another loss, or through more positive changes such as marriage or graduation). By helping the family become aware of the universal nature of stress related to transitions and by building on the fundamental family supports improved in prior sessions, the family can be helped to deal with basic life changes.

For complex questions such as spiritual issues of belonging and faith, the answers are complex. Stage 1 of therapy frequently addresses surface problems, where somewhat simplistic answers or medication can provide hope. In this fourth, spiritual stage of therapy, the issues, in addition to being complicated, are frequently without answers.

Many families face the reality that family members have disabilities, handicaps, inbred illnesses, and other difficulties that are only modifiable and not changeable. A basic dilemma for all families is to know which human limitations and attitudes are changeable, such as the ability to promote a life-affirming attitude, and which universal life challenges, such as death, are unavoidable.

Celia Falicov (1983, 1988, 1995) stresses the use of a cultural lens in all stages of family therapy, as well as life transitions. She stresses four key comparative parameters:

1. how the family lives and fits in with the environment;
2. where the family members come from and how they blend into the current main culture;
3. the preferred family organizational patterns;
4. the cultural patterning of family developmental transitions.

The main point is that these parameters are discussed at all four stages of family therapy, not as a separate topic of curiosity. If the therapist has a cultural awareness and interest, then the family's own beliefs and practices are better understood and the need for change, or not, is clarified regarding life transitions. The reason for emphasizing cultural concerns in this chapter is that many families in stage 4 work introduce a fuller discussion of limitations in life including cultural, financial, gender, and biological issues. In stage 4, these considerations take on a more philosophical perspective compared to the problem-oriented, family organization, or personality aspects discussed during the earlier stages of therapy.

> Felipe, now 19, was first seen with his family at the age of 13. His father, a successful Mexican businessman, had just died in an auto accident. Felipe and his family were struggling. The mother, an Anglo, had moved the family from Mexico to Southern California. Felipe described numerous cultural factors as he moved through stages 1–3 of therapy. He had to adjust to learning English instead of Spanish; he had to get used to the American culture, which seemed colder than the Latino culture; he was angry about

Mexican laws that took money from his mother; and he had to adjust to being considered the best at soccer primarily because of his Mexican training and heritage. Felipe had learning disabilities as well as an attention deficit disorder. His ADHD was successfully treated with Ritalin. His gregarious personality and athletic ability, both similar to his father's, helped compensate for his limitations.

As Felipe finished high school, not only was he faced with an emancipation transition, but he was also beginning to accept his biological limitations, the deeper impact of not having a father, and the complexity of his mixed Mexican-American influences. The mother remarried an Anglo and Felipe has decided to leave California. Felipe has gone to Mexico City to live and study.

☐ Spiritual Support Systems

As the family reflects on the complexity of universal life challenges, losses, and possibilities, as well as clinical problems and transitions, it is helpful to review the spiritual support systems that are potentially available. The following is a review of Fleischman's (1990) 10-point spiritual outline regarding overlapping religious and psychotherapeutic topics. Examples are presented where the spiritual principle has become apparent because of a family or individual impasse. In the transitional and spiritual stage of therapy, however, these spiritual topics are also discussed as universal truths, paths to improve the quality of life, and as guidelines for enhancing a feeling of well being.

The author first became acquainted with Fleischman when he gave a lecture at the American Psychiatric Association meetings about his book *The Healing Spirit: Explorations in Religion and Psychotherapy* (1990). At the time I had attended a number of psychopharmacology lectures and scientific presentations and felt reassured when I was able to put such knowledge in the context of spiritual and universal life issues for the family.

Fleischman's spirituality, although based on religious beliefs, does not follow religious scriptures or a particular religion. Instead, his work emphasizes the overlap in psychotherapy and spirituality, with spirituality defined as life-affirming awareness and connectedness to other people and the environment. Compared to scientific research, Fleischman defines spirituality as a search for meaning rather than a search for cause and effect. As he points out, spiritual issues can be a context for problem-solving and, as reflected in the outline of this book, spiritual issues are usually dealt with later in therapy after surface problems, organizational issues, and personality rigidities are addressed. In a sense, the therapeutic process helps the family members eventually address higher-level problems that reflect universal human dilemmas.

Fleischman's 10 areas of spirituality within psychotherapy are:

1. witnessed significance
2. lawful order
3. affirming acceptance
4. calling
5. membership
6. release
7. worldview
8. human love
9. sacrifice
10. meaningful death.

Fleischman points out that within the spectrum of each of these areas there are potential abuses: on the one hand, presenting the principles in an extreme, dictatorial way or, on the other hand, allowing the patient to develop an extreme or distorted internal version of the principle.

Psychopharamacology, by helping family members deal with the previous questions of surface problems, organizational rigidities, and personality rigidities, permits the family to more fully address the life challenges and spiritual issues that they face. Even in religious rituals throughout time, drugs and alcohol have been used to help people submit to larger community and spiritual issues and reduce cognitive processes that might interfere (see Scotton, Chinen, & Battista, 1996).

Witnessed Significance

Witnessed significance refers to the therapy process where the therapist can offer listening, appreciation, and "mirroring" to the family. This process is somewhat similar to the religious concept of being aided by a benevolent higher power. Certainly, in early development children require this experience of feeling attended to, in order to develop a healthy self-esteem.

> In a family situation that reflected the lack of witnessed significance, Allan, a college student, presented with panic attacks. The father had expected Allan to go to Harvard University and then to follow in the father's successful professional path. The son felt that his inner thoughts, which included spiritual symbols, were taboo; these inner thoughts also included feelings of criticism toward the father and eventually sexuality. The patient had developed a system where he acted "like a puppet" to fit his family's expectations and hide his inner thoughts and feelings.
>
> At the prospect of admitting and expressing such feelings, which in therapy eventually had numerous vivid images, the patient felt like he was drowning and suffocating. The therapy process provided an antidote to this

history by initiating the missing recognition of the patient's inner life. The process of therapy began with addressing the panic attacks and the family involvement. Both parents, who were divorced, and a sibling were included in the therapy process. The father hoped for a quick cure through medication or behavioral therapy; the mother was more supportive toward an inner psychological life. On the other hand, the mother wanted the patient to stay with her for protection and support.

The initial problems were complicated by an eventual disclosure of obsessions and compulsions that appeared to magnify Allan's distress. Paxil was included in the treatment. As the patient became more aware of the issues and more cognizant that the parents might not be able to provide the needed mirroring, appreciation, and listening, he began to expand these experiences outside of the therapy arena. Several years into the therapy, he is still struggling socially and professionally but has graduated from college, lives independently, and has a regular job and some friends. The therapy provided the witnessing missing in the parenting process.

As Fleischman points out, the extreme perversion of "witnessed significance" would be a patient's having delusions of joining with an all-powerful god or having a delusional inflation (manic or narcissistic) of her own importance. The crucial point is that whatever the life challenge or developmental issue, whether it is graduating from college, getting married, or facing an illness or death, there is a universal need to be appreciated, recognized, and understood.

Witnessed significance is especially valuable in stage 1 therapy, where a sense of comfort and hope are provided by the therapist, as well as in stage 2 work where listening is enhanced. Usually, however, a more formal discussion of the universal need for "witnessed significance" and how the family can maintain listening, appreciation, and support after the therapy ends takes place in stage 4.

Lawful Order

Lawful order is a basic sense that the world, family, or therapy is safe and has some predictable progression greater than simple limits or rules. Such a concept would be an antidote to thinking of the universe as absurd.

> A family illustrating the lack of lawful order and a need for such order to be established, included a high school student, Jason. In addition to having a learning disability, Jason was faced with the facts that his mother was ill and that his father was in jail. Jason continually had to face his impulses to use drugs to self-medicate. Jason's superstitions and addictions appeared to be his own misguided attempt for lawful order. In the therapy, a grandmother was enlisted to help provide family leadership and a sense of safety in the family.

In every family, even after basic family problems are solved, there is a universal life question about how to face a world that can seem, or be, unsafe. The process of therapy can provide a feeling of safety and, at the fourth stage of therapy, these issues are literally discussed as spiritual questions.

The concept of "lawful order" is especially important in stage 1 and 2 of family therapy. The therapist reassures the family that family members will not be hurt. The family is also encouraged in stage 2 to develop an organizational system that promotes safety and security. In stage 3 dangerous personality characteristics are modified. In stage 4 the universal question of safety and security is addressed.

Affirming Acceptance

In this area, impulses and drives are integrated into a unified sense of mind and direction. Most religions have some way to help individuals and families to control sexual and aggressive impulses, for example. In the previous chapter on personalities, one method of addressing an overly aggressive or overly sexual person would be to explore the spectrum of that quality and to integrate aspects of the personality that exhibit propriety or restraint. The perversion of this concept is a sense of being entitled to express all feelings. The opposite perversion is extreme punishment for inner thoughts or impulses.

> A clinical example illustrating a lack of affirming acceptance is Rick, who was mentioned earlier in this chapter. Rick was unable to control his sexual impulses and, in fact, this symptom helped him understand experientially his prostitute mother and helped correct, at least fleetingly, a sense of not feeling important. Rick felt affirmed through sex. He only began therapy after his wife threatened and eventually got a divorce because of her inability to deal with his symptoms.
>
> Partly motivated to preserve a healthy relationship with his two children, Rick endured a therapeutically monitored depression as he reviewed his childhood and the origins of his symptom. Currently, the patient, with the help of medication and sexual addiction groups, has been able to control excessive sexuality and has established more personal friendships with women. With Rick, intimate sex and obsessive sex were distinguished during the personality phase of therapy (stage 3); all families, as a universal theme, must address the issue of somehow incorporating strong feelings and human impulses.

In this particular situation, antidepressants helped Rick tolerate the depression that was part of the therapy process. In addition, Lithium was used to help control sexual impulses. The patient is now dealing with fathering issues and intimacy issues, as well as trying to base his professional advancement on genuine interests. As mentioned earlier, he is asking questions about the meaning of his life and other spiritual matters.

Calling

Calling is the need for feeling useful and connected. At one end of this spectrum when a person feels almost a messianic mission, it may be hard to tell whether there is a delusional component. Clearly, manic or paranoid delusions of a calling would be a perversion of this concept, and referring to one's calling as based on past lives would also be difficult to understand, literally.

> A college student, Itzak, was treated for panic and depression. Other members of his family had undergone previous treatment for various developmental problems. Itzak felt directionless. He was longing for an "inner spiritual truth" to dictate his path as an antidote to feeling micromanaged as a child. While waiting for the muse to strike, Itzak spent most of his time vegetating in front of the television eating sweets, which resulted in health problems and did not improve his state of mind.
>
> Medication (Prozac) was used to control his depression and obsessional thinking and helped him tolerate the discussion of how to combine science and religion, as well as strategic versus naturalistic ways of establishing a calling. Always interested in religion and spirituality as a theme, this young man eventually joined a yeshiva in Israel and, although one might ask to what extent his mission has been internalized, he has been able to become functional and productive.

Again, the clinical situation illustrates a problematic lack of calling and a struggle that all families have for helping family members to feel useful and connected. In this particular example, this rather indolent young man became active and productive as he became educated in helping others (in this case other young people) in a religious context.

"Calling" as well as the next category, "membership," are especially important for stage 2 therapy where family roles and connections are emphasized. Stage 4 addresses the question of how family members' ongoing connections with the community can be maintained after therapy stops.

Membership

By membership, Fleishman refers to a person's feeling that she is inside of history—that she belongs to a group or community or has a basic sense of affiliation. Fleishman distinguishes membership from a calling, pointing out that membership has a particular time and place. As in the other categories, the perverted version would be exemplified by the extreme position, in this case, cults or paranoid hate groups.

> I have been working with Gregory, a 12-year-old with multiple emotional and developmental problems. In addition to attention deficit problems and a tendency toward violence, Gregory had no friends and struggled in a family where the father was very critical about his difficulties.
>
> This patient benefited from a combination of medications including Ritalin for ADHD, Risperdal and Depakote for impulse control, and Paxil for anxiety and depression. One saving experience was that he felt a sense of membership in his religious community and especially, as he recently prepared for and successfully completed his Bar Mitzvah. He became absorbed in the meaning of his torah portion and relished Jewish symbols such as his talis and Star of David. The actual Bar Mitzvah appeared to help him find a way to create social contacts and feel special.

Release

Release refers to the acceptance of universal paradoxes and the intrinsic difficulties in relationships. This concept is somewhat like the serenity prayer, in which a person controls the controllable and accepts that, to survive life, it is necessary to surrender to uncontrollable forces. Again, to point out the extremist or dysfunctional view, individuals who feel total submission and depression as a way of adjusting to life's difficulties demonstrate a maladaptive exaggeration of the point.

> I have worked with two different women regarding fertility problems, both when they were around the age of 50. Charlotte accepted the loss of not having children and went through a moderate depression as she accepted her professional teaching career and friendships as the fulfilling elements of her life rather than children. Interestingly, Charlotte became an expert on fertility issues and also in helping other women deal with this loss.
>
> In a contrasting situation, Diane became obsessed with the possibilities of implanting an embryo in her uterus despite being in her 50's. All meaning in life seemed to fade away in contrast to this obsession. Although such persistence is admirable, even Diane would have to accept that her child did not come in a natural way and time in her life.

"Release" is especially important in stage 3 personality work when individual family members or the family as a whole seeks relief from excessive attempts at control. The more philosophical form of this question is discussed as the therapy draws to a close.

Worldview

This concept is the closest to "pure religion" and reflects the individual's need for a sense that the world is whole, meaningful, coherent, and sacred. This worldview would be polarized with a more narcissistic, self-oriented, pessimistic point of view. Worldview also implies a sense of continuity even as generations come and go.

> A clinical situation that illustrates the lack of a worldview was provided by a college student, Ron, who succumbed to an alcohol and heroin addiction. Ron's ideal fantasy was to be alone in a cabin with marijuana and perhaps a computer so that he could generate income through Internet investments. Inundated by feeling left out of his family and traumatized by a teenage accident, Ron only gradually began to make human contact as he cried about the unfairness and neglect of his family.
>
> The progression of Ron's therapy was slow. Over a 2-year period I did my best to therapeutically support and agree with Ron's point of view, even though it was somewhat antisocial. After building trust, Ron was able to tell the childhood story of his father's giving his brother a special gift, but leaving Ron out. The previously suppressed sadness and rage that were unleashed captured lifelong feelings that had dominated Ron's existence. Ron's lifestyle and attitudes are at the extreme of not having a worldview, but the therapy process has helped him move in that direction.

The concept of "worldview" involves the family's moving beyond day-to-day experiences to contemplate the universe. This concept is relevant to stage 3 personality work where the "spiritual self" might be polarized with the "practical self." Ron had an "alienated self" and an underrepresented "trusting self."

Human Love

This concept is the antithesis of self-absorbed and pathological narcissism. It represents the human capacity for empathy in caring for another. Fleischman points out that human love is often confused with sex and that therapy itself can become an addiction as patients search for love. The concept of human love is also an antidote to the common experience of ambivalence. As Miriam Polster (1992) points out in her book regarding feminine heroism, the heroic ideal of caring in relationships is in contrast to military heroes who are solitary and silent.

> In a clinical example illustrating narcissism instead of human love, Linda, a woman who had married a somewhat older professional, described her anger at having to take care of him as his health declined. Linda described her resentment at having to support her husband financially, which was

very different from her original plan. Therapeutic help for Linda included my compassion for her sense of suffering and my concern that her frustration and anger were destroying her life (she was unable to utilize direct personality confrontation).

The concept of "human love" is especially important for establishing the connections of stage 2 and for correcting excessive narcissism in stage 3. The question of enhancing "well-being" through love and charity becomes a general issue for stage 4.

Byrum Karasu (1999) describes two aspects of spiritual concerns: "soulfulness" and "spirituality." Soulfulness refers to the love of others, of work, and of belonging. Spirituality refers to the belief in the sacred, in unity, and in transformation. Soulfulness is similar to Fleischman's human love, and spirituality is similar to Fleischman's worldview concept. The concept of love is more easily incorporated into all the stages of family therapy that have been presented, compared to worldview, which places the entire therapy in a perspective of being paradoxically extremely important, and yet insignificant at the same time.

Sacrifice

Sacrifice refers to choosing what is less comfortable in order to fulfill a deeper and more profound demand. This concept refers to the inevitable suffering that occurs in human existence and can help such suffering have more meaning. The distorted extreme of this concept includes certain organizations demanding an excessive percentage of income, as if for protection. Also, certain massacres have been pervertedly reframed as sacrifices.

> In an interesting clinical vignette regarding sacrifice, an outstanding professional family gave 15% of their income to various charities. In addition, the parents took their children to a homeless shelter where they were made sensitive to the needs of the less fortunate. Unfortunately, because of the need to be a perfect family in all ways, including providing charity, the family was joyless and constantly under stress. The family's sense of inevitable suffering had become extreme and therapy experiments were devised to create immediate joyful sensations and pleasure, as an antidote.

Meaningful Death

In the background of every clinical and family situation is the knowledge of one's mortality. Religions and therapy try to create a way to confront, understand, and incorporate the concept of death into daily life. One basic philosophical point of view is to focus on life enhancement even as one faces aging. The counterproductive extremes of this concept would include, on one end, being indifferent to or in denial about the inevitability of death or, on the other end, being constantly phobic or depressed about death.

> One elderly patient, Alice, had recently read the book *A Map to the End of Time* by Ronald Manheimer (1999). Alice felt that the philosophical concepts presented helped her with the process of aging. These included concepts of belonging and connectedness, the value of reviewing the story of her entire life, and the value of humor as a humanizing and dignifying force. Alice also described the philosophical split described by Manheimer between theoretical philosophy and practical philosophy, which parallels one theme in this book between theoretical and problem-solving schools of family therapy.
>
> In one inspirational clinical example, Denise, a woman in her 70's, went through a difficult divorce from her husband after finding out that he had sexually molested one of their grandchildren. Facing life alone with a personality style that was overly stoical and nonexpressive, Denise went through a depression until she could establish a new support system. She began to take walks with a walking group on the beach, attended musical productions on a regular basis, and joined a psychotherapy group and a literary group where she could share her poetry. The individual therapy has alternated from periods of existential despair about family losses and losses from aging to periods with a full sense of inspirational living day-to-day in a deeply connected way.

In considering the four stages of therapy, it is interesting to note that the more practical problem-solving aspects of therapy usually occur at the beginning. The more spiritual and community-related aspects of therapy are usually addressed far into the therapy after practical problems are less foreground. Considering a continuum from sometimes easily addressed surface symptoms to contextual issues, including universal questions about life and death, can help families avoid the extremes that are present in the family therapy profession, philosophy, and culture.

The therapeutic aim is to help the family bridge both practical problem-solving and contextual, spiritual support. Spiritual principles are valuable for enhancing the safety of stage 1, the connections of stage 2, and the acceptance of paradoxical wants and needs in stage 3. Frequently, families as a whole will favor practical problem-solving over spirituality, or the reverse, and frequently factions within the family will favor one versus the other. Therapy then becomes a dialogic mediation between the two positions, with respect and consideration for each position and numerous conversations considering both points of view. Many families will choose to end therapy after the more practical superficial problems are solved, but the author prefers to give families a choice of proceeding to each deeper stage. All considerations and all decisions and deliberations with the therapist are overt rather than manipulative to promote continued therapy.

A fair question to ask about psychopharmacology is to what extent anti-anxiety agents, antidepressants, or mood and thinking stabilizers can facilitate consideration of spiritual issues. To the extent that medications are needed to maintain flexible organizational and personality functioning, and to the extent that intrusive symptoms can be controlled, many families can consider deeper contextual issues with the help of medication. Again, medication would be a topic for therapeutic debate within the family. A more difficult debate occurs when medications are seen as optional, for example, when there is a grief reaction that is not clearly a clinical depression (see Shuchter, 1986). Certainly, the medication would be misused if it short circuits facing difficult feelings and thoughts. On the other hand, if the medication can help a family feel more comfortable and better able to deal with loss issues, then it might be helpful.

Spiritual principles are relevant to all stages of family work, but are more foreground in stage 4. The staging dimension permits an integration and bridging all the way from practical problem-solving to spirituality by continually shifting the focus back and forth between these two extremes, while still honoring the family therapy process toward deeper universal transitions, life challenges, and the experience of well-being.

CHAPTER 7

What are Supervision and Therapist Issues in Helping Families?

As a therapist works with families, she needs to consider the stages of therapy in a dynamic way. That is, she is aware of sensitively managing and moving a family forward and is also aware of the personal meaning the family's issues may illicit in her own thoughts and feelings. The therapist may feel more comfortable dealing with some foreground or background issues and some stages than with others. This awareness helps mitigate against countertransference problems. The supervisor can help the therapist understand her interaction in four main areas, which parallel the stages of therapy.

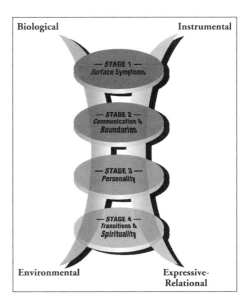

Biological

Instrumental

— STAGE 1 —
Surface Symptoms

— STAGE 2 —
Communication & Boundaries

— STAGE 3 —
Personality

— STAGE 4 —
Transitions & Spirituality

Environmental

Expressive-Relational

123

Surface issues. The therapist will need help in determining how to reduce suffering in the family and will present to the supervisor troubleshooting questions on how to handle practical matters, such as self-destructive behaviors, difficult diagnostic questions, and how to deal with family members who are reluctant to participate in therapy (see Resnikoff, 1981).

Communication and boundaries. The next level of supervision would be to help the therapist join the family in a flexible way. Just as with families, therapists can be either overly engaged or underengaged; therapists are generally helped by practicing flexibility along this dimension. The general communication and boundary style of the therapist should be considered.

Personality issues. The therapist will occasionally have personality issues that are either similar to personality issues in the family or polar opposites. It is important for the therapist to be aware of these personality dynamics and be sensitive to her own internal process to be able to use this information to assist the family rather than be overly identified in a nonproductive way.

Transitional and spiritual issues. The therapist will have her own developmental/transitional and spiritual issues that resonate with the family. Once again, by increasing her awareness of such issues, the therapist is in a better position to assist families. An effective therapist must recognize distorted or biased personal feelings misapplied to family therapy (countertransference) in order to clearly observe and address the family's concerns.

In addition to cognitively addressing her own reflection of the issues in each stage of family therapy, the therapist must also understand her interactional experience with the family at each phase of therapy. Also just like the treatment family, the therapist at each phase of therapy needs to address instrumental versus expressive-relational and biological versus environmental spectrums within herself.

Another supervision consideration is the extent to which the therapist identifies with a particular teacher or school of thought, and how to integrate that preference with other teachers and other points of view. For example, the author identifies with Erving Polster, and that mentoring process will be discussed later in this chapter.

In all these areas, the basic teaching principle is to increase flexibility and awareness. The supervision process duplicates a therapy staging process, but the therapist's "problem" is the clinical situation itself.

Over the last 2 years in private practice, the author has led a supervision group for psychologists that demonstrates these principles. The four psychologists, Mike, Jeff, Linda, and Irene, were originally in a 1-day training seminar. The group has participated in several teaching formats.

Each member of the group has used the cartoon exercise from McClendon (1983) to describe themselves interacting with a clinical family. This exercise encourages discussion of therapist repetitive patterns (or opposite patterns) at each of the four levels:

1. problem-solving,
2. boundary issues,
3. personality issues,
4. transitional/spiritual issues.

The exercise consists of the therapist drawing a situation with a treatment family that illustrates a supervision question. The therapist also draws cartoons illustrating a current personal conflict and a childhood family conflict.

Another supervisory method used in the group was for each participant to present family cases that would then be discussed with regard to the different stages of therapy. A third technique of supervision was to have each of the four psychologists conduct a live videotaped consultation with one of the author's private practice families, during 1-day seminars held for other professionals, and then be supervised using the four layers of supervision.

☐ Supervision Examples

Stage 1 of Supervision: Facing Practical Dilemmas and Surface Issues

> Irene presented a 25-year-old suicidal young man suffering from delusions and isolation. He was abused as a child and was overly involved with the mother, who tended to be protective and nonconfrontational. The mother wanted to correct the previous abuse from the father. The problem for Irene was how to include a "suicide prevention program" along with her main approach of joining the family with intuition and empathy. Irene, a former nun and spiritual teacher turned therapist, disliked having to control or set limits on patients or families, for fear of disrupting empathy and understanding. Evaluating the interpersonal patterning surrounding the symptom helped Irene see that the mother was unwilling to set limits or appreciate the depths of the symptomatic (and personality) problems.

The practical advice was to include a psychiatric evaluation, with the psychiatrist being the "bad cop," and Irene being the "good cop," in order

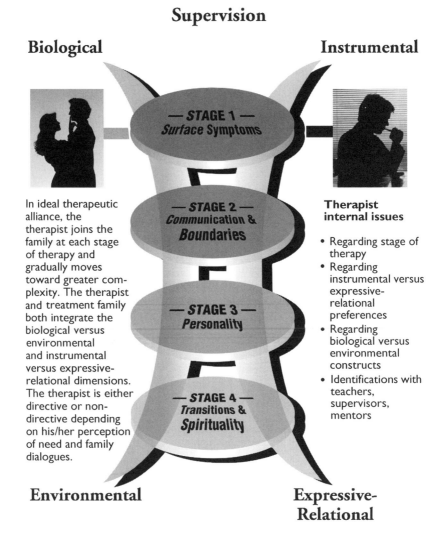

Supervision

Biological   **Instrumental**

— STAGE 1 —
Surface Symptoms

In ideal therapeutic
alliance, the
therapist joins the
family at each stage
of therapy and
gradually moves
toward greater com-
plexity. The therapist
and treatment family
both integrate the
biological versus
environmental
and instrumental
versus expressive-
relational dimensions.
The therapist is either
directive or non-
directive depending
on his/her perception
of need and family
dialogues.

— STAGE 2 —
Communication &
Boundaries

— STAGE 3 —
Personality

— STAGE 4 —
Transitions &
Spirituality

**Therapist
internal issues**

• Regarding stage of
  therapy
• Regarding
  instrumental versus
  expressive-
  relational
  preferences
• Regarding
  biological versus
  environmental
  constructs
• Identifications with
  teachers,
  supervisors,
  mentors

Environmental   **Expressive-
                                              Relational**

FIGURE 7.1.

to present both sides of the dilemma. The group discussion among the four
psychologists focused on the general reluctance to be controlling with families, whether with fees, symptomatic control, or correcting parenting mistakes. This reluctance to be active and controlling was less true in clearly
self-destructive situations. The therapists felt more comfortable mediating
the "good cop/bad cop" splits within the family systems, but the problem discussed was how to deal with the likely positive prejudice of the

therapist in favor of the "good cop." A clinical example from the author's practice was presented, where the family interrupted the progress in therapy with an excessive preoccupation with suicide and suicide prevention. The basic supervision point was to increase therapist flexibility along the continuum of emphasizing practical suicide prevention versus addressing communication and personality issues that might contribute to suicidal feelings.

> In another surface problem situation, Jeff needed help in preserving his therapeutic alliance with a family. The mother in a particular family favored protecting the teenage children from problems and stress, including the stress of being in therapy. Jeff agreed with the father, who believed that the children's school problems and family conflicts should be discussed openly.

The supervision for Jeff was to help him support both parents' points of view, not just the father's, and to work as a mediator. For Jeff, this meant understanding and supporting the mother's opinions regarding the value of taking a child out of school, creating a safe environment, and allowing healing by simplifying the child's world. With this in mind, Jeff was better able to mediate an open discussion between the protective point of view and the more confrontational point of view. The general topic for supervision was surface issues, since the therapist was addressing presenting problems and the family's sequence of events around those problems. (The personality issues could have been the focus.)

In the first case, the therapist was more *laissez-faire* than the family; in the second case, the therapist was more confrontational than the family. The supervision group continued to explore their personal and professional prejudices regarding labeling and controlling surface problems. The basic objective was to have each therapist operate flexibly along a continuum of joining (expressive-relational) versus changing surface phenomenology (instrumental).

Stage 2 of Supervision: Organizational, Boundary, and Leadership Issues

Just as in clinical situations with families, as the surface issues for the therapist were clarified, the therapist's patterns of interpersonal closeness and interpersonal leadership became clear. Each therapist was characterized as having a particular place in the Olson cohesion and adaptability model, used in Chapter 4, which describes a continuum of closeness versus distance (horizontal axis) and a continuum of directiveness versus nondirectiveness (vertical axis). This model classifies the therapist's tendency to be either close or distant with families and also the tendency to be directive

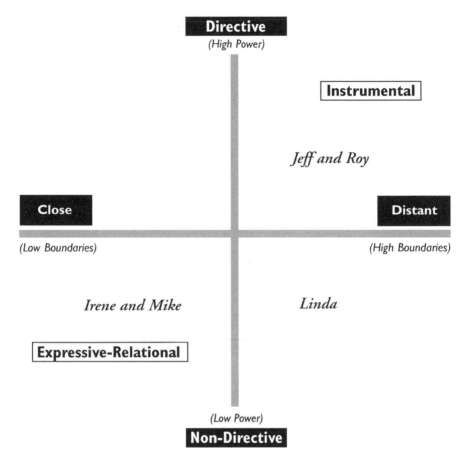

FIGURE 7.2.

or nondirective with families. An instrumental therapist tends toward the directive/distant quadrant; an expressive-relational therapist tends toward the nondirective/close quadrant. The goal of supervision was to increase the range of flexibility in both these arenas.

Irene as a therapist was predominantly close and nondirective, as illustrated in the Olson diagram. In contrast, Irene in her first marriage had felt somewhat distant and was forced to do things for her husband, whom she described as passive. This juxtaposition of opposites from the therapist's professional life to the therapist's personal life is a frequent theme.

Linda was in the distant, nondirective quadrant. Linda felt she needed the structure of psychological testing to help control the excessive stimulation of unstructured family interviews. Although she could give critical feedback and testing results, Linda disliked directing homework or enactments. Interestingly, Linda in her private life felt overly controlled by the needs of her former husband and mother and had difficulty in setting limits with her children. In Linda's situation, her professional boundary issues were duplicated in her personal life.

Jeff was in the more directive, distant Olson quadrant. Jeff tended to use a cognitive, rational approach to evaluate and treat families. Although embedded in a mild-mannered, soft-spoken style, Jeff's main approach was to have a parenting, guiding influence. His supervision was to consider more joining approaches, such as experimenting with stream of consciousness possibilities. In addition, Jeff practiced being more responsive rather than directive. In his personal life, Jeff had rebelled against an overly selfish, controlling father by being soft-spoken and calm. Despite this difference in expressive style, he had retained a potent directive impact on his patients.

Mike, who had a special interest in gay couples' therapy, had an unusual acceptance and empathy for alternative lifestyles. Mike's view was the opposite of his parents. Mike described feeling controlled, however, by patient demands and needs; setting limits was a problem. In this regard Mike was characterized as being in the close, nondirective Olson quadrant. Mike was given help in the form of using the disclaimer that he wanted to be accommodating, but that in his role as a therapist he wanted to be able to confront interpersonal patterns in a therapeutic way. Mike was also helped to mediate polarities within family systems, while understanding that he was biased toward nondirective closeness.

Stage 3 Supervision: Personality and Style Issues for the Therapist

> In one group supervision session, Linda presented a family where the father, recently out of jail for a white-collar crime, manipulated her as well as his family. He insisted on what would be discussed and who would come to a particular session. In the face of the father's charm and insistence, Linda felt powerless.

The general topic at the supervision group meeting was the spectrum of therapists' helplessness and powerlessness, on the one extreme, all the way to situations where the therapists felt empowered, helpful, proud, and able to facilitate change. In this particular supervision group, there was a preponderance of therapeutic support for the "underdogs" in life. All four members had had experiences in their upbringing of feeling overly dominated and controlled. The therapeutic bias for all four members was to promote expression and openness in families without control or manipulation. All four therapists were sensitive to the possibility that therapy can be an abusive process.

As each case regarding personality issues was discussed in the supervision group, the therapist's personality awareness was used to identify personality polarities and to help with considering role reversals or expanding personality rigidities. Mike had personal issues regarding his family's not accepting his homosexuality and had developed a style of secretiveness and shame. Jeff had described a situation where his father was preoccupied with his auto racing hobby and social life and considered Jeff a nuisance. Jeff described never wanting to be as boisterous and controlling as his father, who at times seemed literally manic. Jeff was especially sensitive to control and narcissism issues. Linda described feeling overwhelmed by the emotional needs of her mother and fortunately had a relative who could help her deal with feelings of helplessness. Linda was especially tuned in to issues of helplessness in her clients. Irene had changed from being a spiritual teacher to being a psychotherapist; she was especially sensitive to intuitive and spiritual issues as she connected with her clients. Irene felt she had never had her "hand held" while growing up, and in her therapist role she was extraordinarily supportive and caring. These snapshots of personality issues highlight the complexity of the therapy process but also demonstrate the universal nature of most human concerns.

Understanding one's personality issues is a powerful determinant of successful intervention with a family. Such awareness allows the therapist to proceed with clarity and awareness of possibilities, rather than from a rigid or defensive position.

Stage 4 Supervision: Therapist Transitional and Spiritual Issues

Irene had remarried and could understand first-hand the issues of blended families and remarriage. Linda had recently divorced and was experiencing the emancipation issues of children in their 20's. Jeff was starting a new family and launching his private practice; personally and professionally he was especially interested in fathering issues. Mike had selected a life partner; despite some recent relationship turmoil he continued to establish a satisfying social network, traveled extensively, and had a successful professional career as a psychotherapist. Each therapist had a special knowledge and insight into their particular transition in life. The supervision topic was to make sure that each therapist did not impose his or her own personal transitional coping styles onto treatment families; instead, knowledge and experience were seen as potential facilitators for helping others.

All four therapists attended a 1-day workshop on the Fleischman healing and spirituality model described in Chapter 6; the issues presented there were reviewed in a personal way for each therapist. The group especially turned to spiritual inspiration when helping families with catastrophic, unnatural deaths related to drug overdoses, cancer, accidents, AIDS, or murder.

☐ Illustrations from the Author's Practice

My own therapist issues at each of the four stages of therapy also illustrate and clarify the importance of self-awareness. The complexity of exploring the four stages of therapy together with the four stages of supervision underscores the multilayered aspects of the therapeutic process. Although such complexity makes it more difficult to scientifically study therapy efficacy, I believe that awareness of complexity is crucial for effectively helping families.

Overall, by temperament and style, I am in the directive and distancing quadrant of the Olson model. In contrast, most of my interventions are based on intuition, and I usually am perceived as kind and caring. The more controlling, distancing style is more like my father and less like my mother, who was the more emotional storyteller in the family. Through life experience, therapy, and training, I have become more flexible and have expanded the expressive-relational parts of my personality. Now in my 50's, I am also more attuned to aging and spiritual issues. Over the years, I have used various colleagues as supervisors and currently meet once a week with my associate, Deborah Lapidus. We each discuss our clinical dilemmas and give supervision to each other.

Following are examples of clinical cases and my own personal supervision issues.

Stage 1 Supervision: Practical Problem-Solving

Recently, a high-functioning family with a politician father and four educated children came for help regarding their 24-year-old daughter, Marcie, who appeared paranoid and manic. Previously, Marcie had been a successful artist. The whole family, without Marcie, met for two sessions and described their fears and their inability to control Marcie. Marcie had physically assaulted a sister and had verbally attacked the family. When she finally came to a family session, Marcie appeared psychotic. She was pacing; she ridiculed the family, me, and my office. Her speech was rapid and covered numerous topics. She mentioned suicide as well as revenge possibilities. In retrospect, I wondered if I should have seen her alone to avoid the provocation of the family interaction. At the time, I prescribed Depakote and diagnosed the patient as having a "mood instability." I advised the family that hospitalization might be needed if the basic safety of the family became jeopardized. Although Marcie did take one Depakote dose, at home, several hours after the session, she took a kitchen knife and threatened either to kill herself or the family. The police were called but when they arrived Marcie suddenly became peaceful and explained that she was "only joking" to draw attention to her dysfunctional family. A 72-hour hold in the hospital was denied, despite my recommendation, because the patient was not considered dangerous or psychotic at the time.

I felt helpless. Although I had felt confident in my diagnosis and alliance with the family, I had failed to control a potentially dangerous situation despite medication, family limits, and involving the police. I needed practical problem-solving supervision on how to handle my anxious, helpless state, and supervision on alternate ways to be more helpful or effective with the family.

In fact, the police incident did generally calm Marcie and apparently let her know that there were limits. Subsequently, the family allowed Marcie back into the house but told her that she would have to leave if she became verbally combative. Marcie has not yet taken medication or come for therapy, but the family continues, as instructed, to periodically mention to her that they feel she has a treatable mood instability that could benefit from medication and therapy. I have continued to work with the rest of the family to help with other family issues and gradually address the overly fluid, overly emotional nature of the entire family. I can imagine progressing to stages 2 to 4 therapy at some point, but I still feel preoccupied with a potentially dangerous, unstable person who is refusing appropriate treatment. I certainly was able to identify with the family fear and helplessness because I had experienced it firsthand. The family and I resolved to do the best we could and not give up on Marcie; we would both try to improve our effectiveness while realizing our limitations.

Stage 2 Supervision: Boundary and Communication Issues

In a second clinical example emphasizing boundary issues, a dual-profession couple asked for help in dealing with his parents. The parents, part of an ethnically close Jewish family from the East Coast, were upset that the son, Abe, was leaving the family business and home. He planned to live and work on the West Coast. The parents perceived the new wife, Claire, as an enemy trying to create a wedge between the parents and their son. I had the parents come in from the East Coast for three extended sessions over a weekend. I listened to their concerns about the wife and their feelings of loss regarding their emancipating son. I also listened to the son's guilt about displeasing his parents. Abe's family was characterized by a low boundary organization with very directive parents. In therapy, Abe was helped to resist the existing structure of his family.

When Abe and Claire clearly asked for help in setting limits, I decided to support the new marriage and help Abe and Claire label and restrict Abe's parents' disrespect and name-calling toward Claire. In a polite but firm way, visitation and phone call restrictions were placed on the parents; these limits eventually resulted in the parents backing off. Abe and Claire stayed on the West Coast and now have a daughter. Since the boundary conflict with the husband's parents has settled down, the couple has gradually increased intermittent contact with Abe's parents. This couple, over a period of years, has also consulted with me on parenting issues and on issues with Claire's family. Claire's parents were also included in later sessions.

The supervision issue for me was the question: Was I duplicating my own Jewish emancipation issues as a therapist by overly promoting structural boundaries? My own parents did not come to my wedding and had also criticized my non-Jewish wife. I had struggled to set limits in my own life and to deal with my guilt about emancipating. Was I simply acting out my own issues regarding boundaries? After further exploration and examination, my conclusion was that my personal experience actually facilitated my understanding the situation and that my support for the couple underscored their wishes to emancipate and establish appropriate boundaries around their marriage. One of the criticisms of the structural school of family therapy is that "normal" developmental steps are prescribed and imposed on families instead of supporting and honoring intrinsic family dynamics; I was especially clear not to impose my values.

Stage 3 Supervision: Personality Issues

In an informal review of approximately 100 physician families that I had worked with, about 50% of the physicians were predominately rational, controlling, and somewhat obsessive-compulsive. Approximately 25% of the physicians were predominately helpers and "nice" people who would subjugate their own needs to helping patients or other people. The remaining 25% were more outgoing, flamboyant, and self-absorbed. Many of the spouses had opposite personality styles. I can identify with all three personality styles mentioned. With age and experience, as well as personal therapy and supervision, I am, hopefully, more flexible in all three personality styles.

Mary and Joe sought counseling in an effort to reconcile after a marital separation. Mary earned three times the income of Joe. She was the dominant partner and complained about Joe's unreliability. Joe complained about her controlling, depressive, and critical nature. The good news was that she offered stability and wholesomeness that had been lacking in his life, and he offered fun and romance that had been lacking in her life. I initially overly sided, in my mind, with Mary against Joe. I thought of her as the more worthy, admirable member of the couple. In therapy, I didn't act out this excessive side-taking. I did openly reveal my "dilemma" in temporarily siding with Mary as a way to correct this imbalance. I supported the marriage and helped emphasize the mutual healing therapeutic aspects of the marriage. Mary and Joe are still together and have become gradually closer and more intimate, as well as appreciative of their helpfulness to each other.

The personality supervision issue for me was understanding that I admired the wife's sophistication and carefree attitude, qualities that had been missing in my upbringing. I wished to emulate these qualities in my adult personality and could easily identify with these qualities in others. Supervision helped me to avoid the extremes of overly questioning or supporting the marriage; instead, I believe that I was able to primarily follow the wishes of Mary and Joe.

With more experience, I have allowed myself to use such personal reactions and intuitions therapeutically rather than quickly suppress them. The theme for supervision is to explore and develop intuition, reactions, and experience, all used with awareness and maturity, to help in the treatment of clinical families. An instrumental therapist reading this section might say it is better to simply use medication, or behavioral modification, rather than deal with all the complications of getting involved with patients. As outlined earlier, this stance would be the more simple, pragmatic outlook. The other end of the therapeutic continuum would argue that life is intrinsically complex and that people naturally yearn for helpers. Such helpers are human and have vulnerabilities and rigidities similar to the client's. The supervision objective is to help therapists be as flexible, mature, and experienced as possible in order to promote healing through therapeutic personal connections, as well as through instrumental means. In addition, the therapist needs to be aware of timing, that is, when personal connection is helpful and when it is not.

Stage 4 Supervision: Spiritual and Life Transition Concerns

Currently I am in my mid 50's and have two sons in college. I am in my second marriage and have been in the private practice of family psychiatry in La Jolla, California, since 1975. This book has been a summary of my professional experiences, but it will also help structure my future teaching and professional development.

Increasingly, my colleagues have become vulnerable to the process of aging. Recently, some of them have either been ill or have died. The family therapy and gestalt community recently mourned the death of George Sargent, 55. It was a very difficult loss; it was hard for me to reconcile George's vitality and vibrancy with his illness. It has felt especially strange to have several families that were former clients of George's arrive in my office to continue their therapy.

In a second painful situation, a couple presented for help with the husband, a surgeon approximately the author's age, developing Alzheimer's disease. His memory loss, word loss, and emotional deterioration seem to be a personal reminder of the tentative nature of life. Therapists are frequently required to confront life and death issues in a profound way. I was unsure how openly I might share my emotions when the Alzheimer patient described his fantasies of death and the loss of his career as a surgeon. Supervision was needed to clarify what worked for the patient and what worked for me. I needed to understand what would be helpful, what would be distracting, what would be personal, and what would be too personal. Working with his wife forced me to clarify my own fears regarding death and how to cope with the survivor's caretaking role.

☐ Biological Versus Environmental Issues Within the Therapist

I continue to struggle with the spectrum of nature versus nurture. My ideal would be to have a truly integrated mixture of biological and environmental constructs in my work. In fact, depending on the decade, the last conference that I have attended, or the particular client I am seeing, biology or environment seems to be especially foreground. Sometimes I can see traits in my father, son, and myself that seem dramatically genetically based. These genetic qualities include a persistent, rational, functional outlook on life; but at times I share the exuberant temperament of my mother. At other times, my family dynamics and cultural/educational experiences seem more influential. My family dynamics included a dominant, emotional mother and a more passive father. My brother, Don, provided most of the intimate "parenting." My educational opportunities and the ability to have a career that promotes human connection and awareness also seem important for my personal development.

My education and professional experience have been dichotomized and polarized. On the one hand, I have had the scientific background of medical school and my science education, including physiological psychology. Certainly, the recent trends in psychiatry and pharmacology are to establish scientific, reproducible research as well as instrumental cognitive and behavioral models for change. On the other hand, through my own personal family therapy and psychoanalytic therapy, experiences with gestalt therapy, and experiences with the more narrative schools of family therapy, I have been exposed to the humanistic, interpersonal, expressive-relational emphasis for helping people. Although I have not used psychopharmacology for myself, I would be open to medication for my family or myself, if indicated.

☐ Integrating Models of Therapy and Integrating Mentoring Influences

Recently, the author was asked to make a presentation as part of the celebration honoring the careers of Erving and Miriam Polster, leaders in gestalt therapy over the last 40 years and colleagues in La Jolla, California. I began to think how Erv had become my professional parent and how I had emulated many of his professional values, his practice style, and his theoretical stance. In thinking about Erv's conceptualization of a "population of selves" and gestalt methods for integrating personality polarities as they apply to my professional life, I found myself asking, "Am I really a gestalt therapist?" I asked Erv. He pointed out that a gestalt therapist is one who is guided by gestalt therapy concepts that are broader than the stereotypes and slogans by which it is frequently identified. These concepts usually exist on a continuum with other related concepts, which leaves choice for individual therapists to honor their own styles and repertoires.

There are several gestalt continuums Erv has proposed with which I identify:

> **The contact/empathy continuum.** Empathy is the subjective joining with the patient's feelings, and it is an integral part of contact. Gestalt therapists have often shunned the concept of empathy in the belief that it masked differences between therapist and client. For me, therapeutic contact always includes empathy. To be mindful, therefore, of helping the client would not overshadow "real" contact.

> **The past, present, and future continuum.** This continuum includes a very complete historical and developmental exploration, always moving with the patient toward future projections or ideals. This exploration broadens gestalt therapy from its stereotype as a here-and-now therapy and reminds us of the gestalt view of the present as inclusive of remembering and planning.

> **The directive/self-regulatory continuum.** This continuum lets the therapist choose to be directive when good quality contact calls for it, as it may in dangerous or suicidal situations or when giving kind advice

or other forms of a helping hand would further the patient's movement. The gestalt preference for an emerging dialogue or increasing awareness would be background to instructive therapeutic efforts.

The transference/contact continuum. The wariness of psychoanalysis is replaced by openness to actual engagement. Engagement may include the acceptance of positive feelings, as well as negative feelings of the client when they represent true rather than distorted feelings.

The health/pathology continuum of the major character qualities of introjection, projection, confluence, retroflection, and deflection. Appreciating the stylistic benefits of any of these qualities gives the therapist greater choice in assessing their beneficial or harmful consequences.

Awareness/action continuum. Awareness is not to be compulsively sought. Action and good quality contact may sometimes take precedence on the assumption that clarified awareness will occur. If awareness does not come as fully as I would like, the action and good quality contact may well be enough. Sometimes I may even want to diminish awareness, as, for example, in panic attacks and other inassimilable experiences.

Psychopharmacology/personal relationship continuum. Medication is to be included within the gestalt repertoire as a personal support and to help promote both contact and awareness where these are otherwise diminished.

Diagnosis/treatment continuum. Classification is acceptable in the therapeutic experience when it helps plan treatment and facilitate therapist-to-therapist communication. This process risks hierarchical distancing and judgmentalism, so one must also be attuned to the need for equal collaboration on issues.

Political/therapeutic continuum. Political consciousness includes the therapist's representing society's needs for less violence, decreased use of drugs, and greater family commitment, rather than separating the individual's wants and needs from societal pressures.

Polster, following the philosophy of other gestalt pioneers such as Paul Goodman, is able to embrace the full range of these continua, always critical of overly rigid gestalt stereotypes.

Some of Polster's admirable healing powers reflect his personality as well as his integrative theory. He has an ability to listen and validate that is mesmerizing. He can attend in a totally focused, enveloping way, making the other person feel central and understood. Polster can be humble, humorous, and self-effacing in a manner that gives his interventions more credibility and effect. Therefore, his confrontations and critiques are not experienced as controlling or alienating. He has the ability to perceive and articulate paradoxes in almost any clinical situation, sometimes actually playing out dialogic tension between the differing points of view.

I know I cannot match these healing qualities, his high energy, or his professional ambition. He remains an internalized ideal. His impact personally and professionally has been more pervasive than I realize. Once, after a presentation for the American Group Psychotherapy Association in New York, a listener said that my manner, stories, and humor reminded her of her therapist, Isadore From, who had been a strong influence on Polster.

What is the author's view of gestalt therapy? It is not the gestalt stereotypic, charter member, true believer, therapist image. Instead, in addition to the nine continua just discussed, the author sees gestalt therapy as helping clients become self-aware, cognizant of their interactions, and facilitating new experiments for change. This therapy occurs in a context of equal, respectful humans interacting as real people with the therapist avoiding hierarchical superiority. Paul Goodman in *Gestalt Therapy* (Perls, Hefferline, & Goodman, 1951) warned against "splits" in psychotherapy, including:

1. body and mind,
2. self and external world,
3. emotional and real,
4. infantile and mature,
5. biological and cultural,
6. poetry and prose,
7. spontaneous and deliberate,
8. personal and social,
9. love and aggression,
10. unconscious and conscious.

Gestalt stereotypes perpetuate such splits. On the other hand, if such stereotypes are redefined as preferences along flexible continua, they can serve as core theoretical grounding.

In order to clarify issues regarding integration of such splits, here are three examples from current clinical practice, exploring differing professional selves:

> In a family recently seen, two sons, 30 and 32, were living at home with their parents. The 30-year-old son had been panicky; he thought he was "dying" after the breakup of an 8-month intimate romance. He had not dated for the previous 7 years and had anxieties about sex, the girlfriend's moving in, and whether women would accept an allergic skin condition from which he suffered. He was also unable to develop a career, pointing out that even in golf he was frightened of the spotlight and the tension of competition.

I was compassionately attentive to the story presented by both parents and their son. I listened to their theories of the son's hypersensitivity to the girlfriend's betrayal. The patient thought he might never recover and felt "total devastation."

After the first session, I prescribed a combination of an antianxiety/ depression agent (Paxil), a stimulating antidepressant (Wellbutrin), and serotonin-enhancing sleeping pills (Trasodone) to help avoid hospitalization. This was not typical gestalt therapy, but my experience in using medication rescued my "medical self" from the stereotype of psychopharmacology as dehumanizing. I was unsure, diagnostically, whether I was treating a straightforward reactive panic with obsessive features, or a more paranoid/schizoid biochemical and ego problem. My suspicion was the latter. My medical self, diagnosing an illness, felt in contrast to my humanistic, noninterventional, supportive self. I began to think of Erv Polster. He would probably support what I did, directly helping my client, since he also avoids being constrained by an oversimplified notion of gestalt therapy. I reflected that my medical model diagnosis, medical treatment, and taking over was my "psychiatric self," but I was moving cautiously toward a more "classical" gestalt, humanitarian view of the situation, eventually connecting, and hopefully participating in this person's life transition and growth.

Furthermore, using lessons learned from Polster's book, *A Population of Selves*, I began to have my own internal dialogues arguing the technical versus humanistic professional points of view in the treatment of this family. My technical side would argue that my diagnostic, medical knowledge was indeed important. The humanistic side would argue that personal connection was indispensable and that I must be careful not to lose touch with the client. The client in this example also pointed out that a previous psychiatrist had a monotone, and coldly said that the patient had a chemical deficiency; the patient felt this prior therapist had a "sterile office" with a separate entrance and exit. I told myself to stay with the family's unfolding dramatic story and to appreciate the son's fear of professional intrusion. Paradoxically, the patient also had a great need to be understood by a professional.

> In another case, I was asked to evaluate and help a divorcing couple and their 5-year-old son. The father had been accused of inserting objects into his son's rectum, but vehemently denied this accusation (supported by two lie detector tests).

As I began my evaluation, in addition to my compassionate, understanding, professional self, I found myself also being the investigative detective trying to find the truth. I felt like divorce mediator, judge, jury, and representative of the 5-year-old. I was much more of an advocate than my gestalt stereotype would allow.

> Finally, with another client, I felt more like a "classical" gestalt therapist, helping a 36-year old, high-functioning father be more guiding and less power-oriented with his 7- and 5-year olds. He said that controlling, militaristic fathers were a three-generation tradition and asked for help in reducing his excessive parenting power.

At last, here was a more typical therapeutic situation, where self-direction by the patient is in the foreground. Even here, though, I did give some parenting tips and suggested structured exercises to help the father get started in giving his children educational lessons rather than punishment. The therapy addressed the father's difficulties in carrying out this behavioral "experiment." Basically, I felt myself to be joining with the father in enhancing his fathering and, later, the marriage.

Most professionals establish their styles from identifying with significant teachers as mentors, from the orientation of their academic instruction and practical experience. Although Erving Polster has had the most profound impact on my professional identity, I have also benefited from teachers who are expert in neuropsychiatry, as well as therapists who are leading thinkers in the spiritual and humanistic realm. Overall, as has been the theme in the author's recent writing, there is a professional dichotomy in terms of technical, instrumental therapy approaches versus humanistic, relational approaches. I think of myself as basically humanistic but willing to use technical information and instrumental healing methods. Polster as a "charter gestalt member," emphasizing the healing aspects of human connection, has also promoted a broad spectrum of clinical flexibility. I also seek to become more and more capable of integrating the spectrum of technical and humanistic work.

Several other teachers have contributed to my inner professional dialogue, many of whom are quite different from Erving Polster.

On a problem-solving level, I can still picture the transactional analyst Bob Goulding (Goulding & Goulding, 1978; Goulding, 1997) using imagery and deconditioning to help control phobias. His behavioral control methods also included a developmental and dynamic understanding. Similarly, Bill Baak, a family psychiatrist, coached parental discipline using hypnosis principles in a context of developmental understanding. I remember Milton Erickson's purple outfit as he demonstrated directed behavioral change (Haley, 1967). His hypnotic principles were important to many directive family therapy methods. I frequently think of the cognitive therapist Aaron T. Beck when distinguishing what he calls "neurotic" anxiety or depressive thoughts from reality thoughts (Beck & Emery, 1985). Beck's work also includes an understanding of underlying belief systems and experiences (Beck, 1989). Stephen Stahl (2000) and his methods of prescribing psychopharmacology "cocktails" come to mind for treating severe depression (2000); I also think of the neurologist Oliver Sacks' warning as my medical school teacher to consider the whole person and context when considering medical interventions.

On a communication systems level, I think of family therapy teachers such as Mike Solomon (1973, 1977) and Ruth McClendon (Kadis & McClendon, 1998), who enhanced my understanding of escalating family patterns and repeating family political structures. Other family therapy teachers also exposed me to the power of structural and communication manipulations. I think of James Alexander when, in therapy, I initially join and support existing organizational structures.

On a personality level, during medical school I changed my main professional direction from neurophysiology to interpersonal therapies. I remember the family psychiatrist Ed Hornick's dramatic family interviews with teenagers as being inspirational. I recall bioenergetic workshops with Alexander Lowen that helped me get beyond words in experiencing my body. My psychoanalyst, Peter Manjos (4 days a week for 5 years) gave me a new experience of intimacy and closeness that also expanded my professional life in that direction; my brother, Don, and son, David, were also teachers in this regard. In my upbringing, my father was the more cerebral, technical influence, and my mother the more storytelling, expressive influence. My two marriages were to women who enhanced my connectability.

On a spiritual level, the psychoanalyst Paul Fleischman has been an important influence. I have become more aware of advancing age, the life transition of my two sons in college, and wondering what my professional contribution has been. When I am in my 70's, I hope I have as much energy as Erv Polster; and, not unlike Erv, my plan is to continue to work, learn, and experience life to the fullest extent, for as long as possible. Just as children identify with parents and then learn to develop their own perspective from many relationships and experience, clinicians often integrate a core identity along with a population of professional selves; this integration is influenced by many teachers. Such a process requires openmindedness and flexibility in coordinating and using opposite or paradoxical points of view. Erv Polster has been a primary professional parent and introject. I have emulated him and used his teaching as well as his personal lifestyle for inspiration. I have outlined some of my competing professional selves, including behavioral and technical elements, but I find myself drawn back to the complex gestalt dimensions of awareness and contact as a professional and spiritual grounding. Very often, when unsure of a clinical course, I imagine a conversation with Erv discussing the paradoxical aspects of each question. Overall, I see myself as a gestalt family psychiatrist to honor my gestalt self, my family therapy self, and my psychiatric self.

Erv encouraged me like a good parent to learn from other teachers, and gave me a gestalt road map for integrating different professional selves.

☐ Psychopharmacology and the Therapist

Just as patients may attach symbolic meaning to the medication they are taking or its side effects, the therapist can often administer psychopharmacology agents with a bias or with the therapist's own symbolic meaning. One exercise that helps therapists understand their prejudices is to ask them to consider taking a "magic pill" that would cure all ills. To divide the responses along the organization of this book, some therapists would ask for a happy pill that would relieve certain acute anxiety or other mood symptoms (stage 1). Some therapists would ask for a magic pill that would improve the intimacy in their lives and their connection with significant others (stage 2). Some would primarily hope for help with their long-standing temperament issues, such as being able to relieve chronic irritability or a chronic temper problem, or possibly relieving a lifelong negativity or sensitivity problem (stage 3). Some would ask for a magic pill that would reverse the aging process or make the world be or feel like a safer, friendlier place (stage 4). Others may be offended by the concept of a magic pill, possibly because the pill comes from the outside and would imply a dependency that is not desired. There are numerous other reasons why a therapist might not consider medication.

Ronald Pies (1998) and John Gunderson (1998) are two psychiatrists who have discussed transference and countertransference to drugs. On the caretaking continuum, Gunderson points out that psychiatrists frequently want to be "do-gooders" who help out and will be willing to give drugs and extra time and care in order to relieve suffering. Especially with vulnerable, sensitive families or individuals, this generosity can create a sense of false hope and anger when the promised relief is not delivered. The psychiatrist or therapist can then easily criticize the patient or family and see the patient as unmotivated or ungrateful if medication is refused.

A second area of difficulty relates to the extent that the therapist takes on a parental role that would exaggerate the family's or the patient's feeling childish. In the instrumental versus expressive-relational dimension, if the therapist has a compulsion to be parental or directive, the overuse of drugs could be an agent for acting out such domination wishes. In the spectrum of closeness and distance, one extreme attitude in using medication is to think of the family or patient as a scientific specimen with malfunctioning organs or cells to be treated from a distance. In this dynamic, the therapist is operating behind the scientific one-way screen and refusing to see the holistic picture. This phenomenon of the psychopharmacologist not considering the whole person has been emphasized by Oliver Sacks in his books and movies (e.g., 1990, 1995) about the problem of treating symptoms or organic problems out of context.

An opposite problem in the therapist can be an adherence to an extreme spiritual or humanistic principle. In this dogmatic position, the therapist has to have total respect and equality with the patient; any medication would imply a lack of respect and a classification of the patient as being disturbed or disabled. To avoid this inequality, the therapist would avoid medication at all costs and rigidly see herself as supporting and reflecting interpersonal dynamics or subjective experiences. Similarly, in the extreme, some treatment families will overly seek medication, and some treatment families will be totally resistant, creating special pressures on the therapist.

Using the interpersonal personality styles described by Lorna Benjamin (1993) as outlined in Chapter 5, it is useful and interesting to consider the biases and transferences that therapists might have toward psychopharmacology, if they have some of the personality styles noted.

Odd/Eccentric Cluster

Paranoid: a somewhat paranoid therapist might consider drugs toxic, dangerous, and a profit ploy of large corporate interests. The therapist may prefer to work without psychopharmacological help.

Schizoid: a somewhat schizoid therapist might follow diagnostic and formulary prescription guidelines by rote. She might prefer medication treatment to personal involvement with patients.

Dramatic/Erratic Cluster

Borderline: the somewhat borderline therapist may offer drugs as a bribe to keep adoring and loving patients. If the drug does not work, the therapist might become angry and abruptly switch medications.

Narcissistic: the somewhat narcissistic therapist may promote her drug or combined drug regimen as being the best and a reflection of special therapeutic skills. The therapist may become self-attacking if the medication does not work, and may also become angry at the drug.

Histrionic: the somewhat histrionic therapist might try the latest designer antidepressant to show off. The therapist might be excessively concerned about sexual side effects or sexual enhancement potential of the medication.

Antisocial: the somewhat antisocial therapist might be inclined to prescribe drugs mostly for profit or to see research opportunities as vehicles for profit and competitive gain. The therapist might ignore negative side effects of the drug.

Anxious/Fearful Cluster

Dependent: a somewhat dependent therapist might go along with "standard" antidepressants even if she does not personally value the medication. The therapist might also feel that the therapy will not progress without a dependency on psychopharmacology.

Obsessive/compulsive: the somewhat obsessive/compulsive therapist might need detailed research findings on effects and side effects of medication before prescribing. The therapist might seek the "right" medication for total control of symptoms and blame herself if the medication does not work. The therapist might become excessively devoted to drug research.

Negativistic (Passive-aggressive): the somewhat negativistic therapist might inappropriately prescribe too much or too little medication and prematurely switch medications before there is a chance for the drug to work.

Avoidant: the somewhat avoidant therapist might be basically against medications but might prescribe one or two extremely safe, predictable medications.

As a therapist who has worked both with and without psychopharmacology, I am pleased to have available medications that can motivate experimental behavioral changes which can create, at least initially, a sense of hope. I am also pleased that many medications are able to control distracting symptoms sufficiently so that therapy, which would otherwise not be possible, can take place. I am also surprised that over the years more and more families begin therapy asking for medication and that I have to frequently urge caution. Another trend I am aware of is the overuse of medications. For example, many families ask for attention deficit disorder medications for children and adults. Since the diagnosis of attention deficit disorder can be subtle and overly used, it is essential that medication be prescribed carefully and as an experiment or trial of therapy.

In summary, supervision for therapists helping families has all the complications and layers of priority that parallel the actual family treatment.

The challenge of supervision is to honor the therapist's strengths, style, and professional training and expand all of these qualities to include greater flexibility and effectiveness. A special contemporary issue for supervision is helping therapists consider psychopharmacology and facilitating family discussion regarding instrumental versus expressive-relational uses of medication.

Summary and Conclusions

As I contemplate my two and a half decades of family psychiatry and attempt to confront the complexity and paradoxes of treatment, I realize that I frequently rely on intuitive integration, instinct, and experience rather than literally considering one of the dimensions outlined in this book. Sometimes, for example, when conducting a psychopharmacology evaluation incorporating all family members, I have a sense as to the biological vulnerability over several generations and can consider a medication for thinking, mood, anger, or anxiety as outlined in

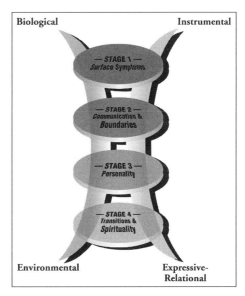

Chapter 5. Almost instinctively, I will know how much joining with the family is needed to form a therapeutic alliance, and how much I can push toward change.

When I began, as an inexperienced therapist, I would focus on the most challenging family member; I now know to start with the easiest connection, sometimes the child, or perhaps even the family pet. Writing this book has helped me realize the constant interplay between paradoxical elements of therapy, not only within the family or couple, but also within myself and in our interaction. I have understood more fully how techniques and psychopharmacology can be used for enhancing awareness and communication without a deliberate push toward change, as well as used for experiments that create alternative possibilities. There is also always the possibility that families heal unrelated to the therapist's acknowledged method, and that such change is due to something entirely different than perceived by the therapist or family.

On the other hand, after I look back on a session or an entire therapy, I can see a method that is teachable and conceptual. Having said that, I would like to review the main dimensional principles that I have outlined, hoping that intuitive, complex, and paradoxical processes in family therapy can be simplified and organized into a pedagogic method that can be replicated.

I have explored four main dimensions or bridges for healing:

1. **Foreground versus background stages of therapy.** Therapy progresses along a developmental continuum and progresses from isolated, narrowly focused, self-absorbing concerns toward a more contextual and worldly view. Paradoxically, the family also moves from complex system concerns regarding symptoms toward individual concerns.
2. **Instrumental versus expressive-relational methods.** Psychological drugs can be useful at both ends of the instrumental versus expressive-relational continuum. Medications can be employed as an instrumental way to help reduce biologically caused target symptoms—those related to genetics or trauma-induced biological changes. At the other end of the continuum, medication can enhance expression, flexible boundaries, temperamental flexibility, and the ability to face life's deeper philosophical, spiritual, and universal loss issues.
3. **Biological versus environmental causes.** To further integrate medication with helping families, each stage of therapy is considered along a nature versus nurture continuum. Treatment for symptoms, boundaries, temperaments, and universal life stresses can be seen as integrating biological and environmental factors, with the help of both scientific research and human experience. It is assumed that most family difficulties, at any stage, have a complex mixture of biological versus environmental elements.
4. **Therapist versus family dimensional interaction.** The therapist works along a continuum of helping efforts in her interaction with the family. The therapist's awareness of her own personal issues and how they resonate with the treatment family's dimensions is crucial. Sometimes the therapist facilitates dialogues between family members

regarding the other three dimensions. (Is the family ready to move to the next stage of therapy? When should medication or technical intervention be considered? What are the biological and environmental resources that might help?) At this end of the continuum, the therapist is the consultant who facilitates discussion and awareness. At the other end, the therapist is the manager who is more instrumental in making decisions or preventing self-destructive phenomena.

Contemporary issues remain that will persist into the next millennium. How can pharmacotherapy for children be monitored to avoid excessive use or administration without psychotherapy? To what extent should therapists represent society's need for greater family commitment and control of drugs and violence? Perhaps therapists should embrace this mission rather than leave it to reactionary political forces. Another important problem is the lack of support for families going through divorce. The current legal system promotes unnecessary adversity and damage to children and parents alike. Yet another issue is health care delivery systems, which have become overly cost-conscious and tend to ignore many of the family contextual issues outlined in this book.

By trying to illuminate and integrate complex theories and clinical issues, I hope I have neither oversimplified the material nor confused the reader. My intent, in the spirit of therapeutic collaboration, is to have therapists and treatment families both use this book to facilitate family change, growth, and satisfaction.

To summarize the integration of pharmacology with family therapy, I have attempted to illustrate medications for biological illnesses along a dimension with medications for enhancing communication and relationship development. This integration involves the full range of this dimension; but instrumental, problem-focused uses of medication are more likely in the earlier stages of therapy when behavioral control is more important; and expressive-relational, communication-enhancing uses of medication are especially relevant in later stages of therapy when communication, personality, and spiritual issues are more foreground.

The dimension of biological versus environmental factors also helps clarify the use of psychopharmacology for enhancing personality flexibility and increasing family interpersonal connection. Medications here are seen as an adjunct to a complex array of therapeutic considerations. Dimensional thinking helps incorporate the diverse and paradoxical forces in helping develop personality flexibility.

An important concept is to have the therapist act as a mediator between family members seeking medication and family members questioning or opposing medication, rather than imposing a psychopharmacology plan on the family. The therapist should also mediate whether medication-augmented problem-solving stops there, or moves on to a longer therapy involving contextual organization, personality, and transition issues. Again, usually one family member favors more therapy, and another favors less.

Another point that I have made throughout this book is how psychopharmacology is much like any family issue. That is, the family's views on medication will demonstrate where they are on every dimension. The discussion about using medication clarifies whether the family thinks the problem is the problem (stage 1), thinks the decision-making is the problem (stage 2), thinks a particular person has a temperament or personality problem (stage 3), or whether life change is the problem (stage 4). Attitudes toward medication also demonstrate instrumental versus expressive-relational biases and biological versus environmental biases. Personality styles and interactional patterns are evident in discussions about considering medication, just as they are with food, sex, and money.

As I write the final paragraphs of this book, the instrumental side of me hopes that I have provided an integration and bridging of psychopharmacology with the four stages of family therapy by using dimensional concepts. I have confidence that therapists and families using this perspective can incorporate the best of divergent professional methods. The expressive-relational side of me feels a combination of pride and humility. As a private-practice family psychiatrist, I feel proud to make a contribution that might help therapists and families to address practical problems and then move on to a higher quality of life. I am humbled by the knowledge that my integrative efforts are built on the shoulders of many brilliant and sensitive clinicians and researchers, to which I add my contribution.

REFERENCES

Akiskal, H. S. (1996). The prevalent clinical spectrum of bipolar disorders. Beyond DSM-IV. *Journal of Clinical Psychopharmacology*, 16(Suppl. 1):4–14.

Akiskal, H. S. & Akiskal, F. (1992). Cyclothymic, hyperthymic, and depressive temperaments as subaffective variants of mood disorders. In A. Tasman & M. B. Riba (Eds.), *Review of Psychiatry*, (pp. 43–62). Washington, DC: Am Psychiatric Press.

Alexander, J. F. & Parsons, B. V. (1982). *Functional Family Therapy: Principles and Procedures*. Carmel, CA: Brooks/Cole.

Anderson, C. M., Reiss, C. J., & Hogarty, G. E. (1986). *Schizophrenia and the Family: A Practitioner's Guide to Psychoeducation and Management*. New York: Guilford Press.

Aron, E. N. (1996). *The Highly Sensitive Person*. New York: Carol Pub.

Baxter, L. R., Phelps, M. E., Mazziotta, J. C., Guze, B. H., Schwartz, J. M., & Selin, C. E. (1987). Local cerebral glucose metabolic rates in obsessive-compulsive disorder. *Arch. Gen. Psychiatry*, 44:211–218.

Beck, A. T. (1989). *Love is Never Enough: How Couples Can Overcome Misunderstandings, Resolve Conflicts, and Solve Relationship Problems Through Cognitive Therapy*. New York: Harper Collins.

Beck, A. T. & Emery, G. (1985). *Anxiety Disorders and Phobias: A Cognitive Perspective*. New York: Basic Books.

Beck, A. T., Rush, A. J., Shaw, B. F., & Emery, G. (1979). *Cognitive Therapy of Depression*. New York: Guilford Press.

Benjamin, L. S. (1993). *Interpersonal Diagnosis and Treatment of Personality Disorders*. New York: Guilford Press.

Bergman, J. (1985). *Pragmatics of Brief Systemic Therapy*. New York: W. W. Norton.

Biederman, J., Faraone, S. V., Hatch, M., Mennin, D., Taylor, A., & George, P. (1997). Conduct disorder with and without mania in a referred sample of ADHD children. *J. Affect. Disorder*, July, 44(2–3):177–188.

Bowen, M. (1978). *Family Therapy in Clinical Practice*. Northvale, NJ: Jason Aronson.

Bowlby, J. (1969). Attachment and loss. In *Volume 1: Attachment*. New York: Basic Books.

Breunlin, D. C., Schwartz, R., & MacKune-Karrer, B. (1997). *Metaframeworks: Transcending the Models of Family Therapy*. San Francisco, CA: Jossey-Bass.

Brown, J. (1979). *Back to the Beanstalk*. La Jolla, CA: Psychology and Consulting, Associated Press.

Cloninger, C. R. (1998). The genetics and psychobiology of the seven-factor model of personality. In K. Silk (Ed.), *Biology of Personality Disorders*, Washington, DC: American Psychiatric Press.

Cloninger, C. R., Svrakic, D. M., & Pryzbeck, T. R. (1993). A psychobiological model of temperament and character. *Archives of General Psychiatry*, 50:975–990.

Cloninger, C. R. & Svrakic, D. M. (1997). Integrative psychobiological approach to psychiatric assessment and treatment. *Psychiatry*, 60(2):120–141.

Coccaro, E. (1998). Neurotransmitter function in personality disorders. In K. Silk (Ed.), *Biology of Personality Disorders*. Washington, D.C.: American Psychiatric Press.

Engel, G. (1977). The need for a new medical model: A challenge for biomedicine. *Science*, 196:129–136.

Falicov, C. (Ed.) (1983). *Cultural Perspectives in Family Therapy*. Rockville, MD: Aspen.

Falicov, C. (Ed.) (1988). *Family Transitions: Continuity and Change Over the Life Cycle*. New York: Guilford Press.

Falicov, C. (1995). Training to think culturally: A multidimensional comparative framework. *Family Process*, 34(4)Dec:373–388.

Fava, G. A., Rafanelli, C., Grandi, S., Conti, S., & Belluardo, P. (1998). Prevention of recurrent depression with cognitive behavioral therapy: Preliminary findings. *Arch. Gen. Psychiatry*, Sep;55(9):816–820.

Feighner, J. (1999). New Research on New Antidepressants. Presentation to San Diego Psychiatric Society, October.

First, M. B. (Ed.). *Diagnostic and Statistical Manual of Mental Disorders*, 4th ed. (1994). Washington, DC: American Psychiatric Association.

Fleischman, P. (1990). *The Healing Spirit*. New York: Paragon House.

Fox, M. (1993). More power to families: Neutralizing the power of medicine. *AFTA Newsletter*, 54:5–9.

Framo, J. L. (1992). *Family of Origin Therapy: An Intergenerational Approach*. New York: Brunner/Mazel.

Frank, J. (1963). *Persuasion and Healing*. New York: Schocken Books.

Gabbard, G. (1996). Introduction. In *Annual Review of Psychiatry*. Volume 15. Washington, DC: American Psychiatric Press.

Glick, I. & Thase, M. (1997). Combined Treatment. In I. Glick (Ed.), *Treating Depression*, Chapter 7. San Francisco, CA: Jossey-Bass.

Goulding, R. (1997). *Changing Lives Through Redecision Therapy*. New York: Grove Allas Publishers.

Goulding, R. & Goulding, M. (1978). *The Power is in the Patient*. San Francisco, CA:TA Press.

Greist, J. (1995). *Obsessive-Compulsive Disorder Casebook*. Washington, DC: American Psychiatric Press.

Griffith, J. & Griffith, M. (1994). *The Body Speaks: Therapeutic Dialogues for Mind-Body Problems*. New York: Basic Books.

Guest, J. (1987). *Ordinary People*. New York: Ballantine Books.

Gunderson, J. & Sabo, A. (1993). The phenomenological and conceptual interface between borderline personality disorder and PTSD. *Am. J. Psychiatry*, Jan;150:1.

Haley, J. (1967). *Advanced Techniques of Hypnosis and Therapy. Selected Papers Of Milton H. Erickson, M. D.* New York: Grune and Stratton.

Haley, J. (1973). *Uncommon Therapy: The Psychiatric Techniques of Milton H. Erickson, M. D.* New York: W. W. Norton.

Hoffman, L. (1981). *Foundations of Family Therapy: A Conceptual Framework For Systems Change*. New York: Basic Books.

Hoffman, L. (1990). Constructing Reality: An Art of Lenses. *Family Process*, 29:1–12.

Hogarty, G. & Flesher, S. (1999). Practice principles of cognitive enhancement therapy for schizophrenia. *Schizophrenia Bulletin*. 25:693–708.

Hogarty, G., Kornblith, S. J., Greenwald, D., DiBarry, A. L., Cooley, S., Ulrich, R. F., Carter, M., & Flesher, S. (1997). Three-year trials of personal therapy among schizophrenic patients living with or independent of family, II: Effects or adjustment of patients. *Am J. Psychiatry*, Nov;154:1504–1513.

Imber-Black, E. & Roberts, J. (1992). *Rituals for our times: Celebrating healing and changing our lives and relationships*. New York: Harper Collins.

Jamison, K. R. (1995). *Unquiet Mind*. New York: Random House.

Janowsky, D. (1999a). Stimulants and antidepressants: Positive regard toward therapy, personal communication.

Janowsky, D. (1999b). Therapist and patient personality characteristics and the nature, quality, and outcome of psychotherapy: Focus on the Myers Briggs type indicator. In D. Janowsky (Ed.), *Psychotherapy Indications and Outcomes*, Washington, DC: Am. Psychopathological Association.

Jensen, P. S., Mrazek, D., Knapp, P. K., Steinberg, L., Pfeffer, C., Schowalter, J., & Shapiro, T. (1997). Evolution and revolution in child psychiatry: ADHD as a disorder of adaptation. *J. Am. Acad. Child Adolescent Psychiatry*, Dec, 36:1672–1679.

Judd, L., et al. (1996). Socioeconomic burden of subsyndromal depressive symptoms in major depression in a sample of the general population. *Am. J. Psychiatry*, Nov 153; 11:1411–1417.

Judd, L., et al. (1998). A prospective 12-year study of sub-syndromal and syndromal depressive symptoms in unipolar major depressive disorders. *Arch. Gen. Psych.*, 55(8):694–700.

Kadis, L. & McClendon, R. (1995). Couples and marital therapy. In B. Sadock & H. Kaplan (Eds.), *Comprehensive Textbook of Psychiatry*, 6th Ed. Baltimore, MD: Williams & Wilkins.

Kadis, L. & McClendon, R. (1998). *Concise Guide to Marital and Family Therapy*. Washington, DC: Am. Psychiatric Press.

Karasu, T. B. (1999). Spiritual psychotherapy. *Am. J. of Psychotherapy*, Spring, 53;2:143–162.

Keller, M., McCullough, J., Klein, D. N., Arnow, B., Dunner, D. L., Gelenberg, A. J., Markowitz, J. C., Nemeroff, C. B., Russell, J. M., Thase, M. E., Trivedi, M. H., & Zajecka, J. (2000). A comparison of Nefazodone, the cognitive behavioral-analysis system of psychotherapy, and their combination for the treatment of chronic depression. *The New England Journal of Medicine*, 342:1462–1470.

Knutson, B., Wolkowitz, O., Cole, S., Chan, T., Moore, E., Johnson, R., Terpstra, J., Turner, R., & Reus, V. (1998). Selective alteration of personality and social behavior by serotonergic intervention. *Am. J. Psychiatry*, 155(3):373–379.

Kramer, P. (1993). *Listening to Prozac*. New York: Viking.

Kramer, P. (1997). *Should You Leave*? New York: Simon and Schuster.

Lebow, J. (1997). The integrative revolution in couple and family therapy. *Family Process*, Mar, 36;1:1–17.

LeDoux, J. (1996). *The Emotional Brain*. New York: Touchstone Simon & Schuster.

Linehan, M. (1993) *Cognitive-Behavioral Therapy for the Borderline Personality Disorder*. New York: Guilford.

LoPiccolo, J. & LoPiccolo, L. (1978). Handbook of Sex Therapy. New York: Plenum Pub.

McClendon, R. (1983). *Chocolate Pudding and Other Approaches to Intensive Multiple-Family Therapy*. Palo Alto, CA: Science and Behavior Books.

McDaniel, S., Hepworth, J., & Doherty, W. (1995). Medical family therapy with somanticizing patients: The co-creation of therapeutic stories. *Family Process*, 34;3:349–361.

McElroy, S. L. (1999). Psychiatric features of 36 men convicted of sexual offenses. *J. Clin. Psychiatry*, June, 60:6.

McElroy, S. L., Phillips, K. A., & Keck, P. E., Jr. (1994). Obsessive compulsive spectrum disorder. *J. Clin. Psychiatry*, 55(Suppl):33–51.

McEwen, B. S. (1997). Possible mechanisms for atrophy of the human hippocampus. *Mol Psychiatry*, May;2(3):255–262.

Manheimer, R. J. (1999). *A Map to the End of Time*. New York: W. W. Norton.

Michels, R. (1996). Can Biology and Psychoanalysis be Integrated? Presentation to San Diego Psychiatric Society, February, San Diego, CA.

Michels, R. (1997). Psychotherapeutic approaches to the treatment of anxiety and depressive disorders. *J. Clin. Psychiatry*, 58(Suppl);13:30–32.

Miklowitz, D. & Goldstein, M. (1997). *Bipolar Disorder, A Family Focused Treatment Approach*. New York: Guilford Press.

Miller, J. B. (1991). *Women's Growth in Connection*. New York/London: The Guilford Press.

Miller, J. B. & Stiver, I. P. (1997). *The Healing Connection*. Boston: Beacon Press.

Miller, M. V. (1995). *Intimate Terrorism*. New York/London: W. W. Norton & Company.

Minuchin, S. (1974). *Families and Family Therapy*. Cambridge, MA: Harvard University Press.

Minuchin, S. & Fishman, C. (1981). *Family Therapy Techniques*. Cambridge, MA: Harvard University Press.

Minuchin, S., Rosman, B. L., & Baker, L. (1978). *Psychosomatic Families*. Cambridge/London: Harvard University Press.

Moltz, D. A. (1993). Bipolar disorder and the family: An integrative model. *Family Process*, 32:409–423.

Olson, D. H. (1986). Circumplex model VII: Validation studies and FACES III. *Family Process*, 25:337–351.

Olson, D. H., Sprenkle, D. H., & Russell, C. S. (1979). Circumplex model of marital and family systems I. Cohesion and adaptability dimensions, family types, and clinical applications. *Family Process*, March 18(1):3–28.

Papolos, D. & Papolos, J. (1999). *The Bipolar Child*. New York: Broadway Books.

Perls, R., Hefferline, R., & Goodman, P. (1951). *Gestalt Therapy: Excitement and Growth in the Human Personality*. New York: Julian Press.

Perugi, G., Akiskal, H. S., Ramacciotti, S., Nassini, S., Toni, C., Milanfranchi, A., & Musetti, L. (1999). Depressive comorbidity of panic, social phobic, and obsessive-compulsive disorders re-examined: Is there a Bipolar II connection? *J. Psychiatry Res.*, 33(1):53–61.

Pies, R. (1998). *Handbook of Essential Psychopharmacology*. Washington, DC: American Psychiatric Press.

Pinsof, W. (1995). *Integrative Problem-Centered Therapy*. New York: Basic Books.

Pittman, F. (1989). *Private Lies: Infidelity and the Betrayal of Intimacy*. New York: W. W. Norton.

Polster, E. (1987). *Every Person's Life is Worth a Novel*. New York: W. W. Norton.

Polster, E. (1995). *A Population of Selves*. San Francisco, CA: Jossey-Bass.

Polster, E. & Polster, M. (1973). *Gestalt Therapy Integrated*. New York: Brunner/Mazel.

Polster, E. & Polster, M. (1999). *From the Radical Center: The Heart of Gestalt Therapy (Collected Writings)*. Cleveland, OH: Cleveland Gestalt Institute Press.

Polster, M. (1992). *Eve's Daughters: The Forbidden Heroism of Women*. San Francisco, CA: Jossey-Bass.

Rapoport, J. (1999a). New Research on Childhood Schizophrenia from the NIMH. Presentation American Psychiatric Association, May, Washington, D.C.

Rapoport, J. (1999b). Progressive cortical change during adolescence in childhood onset schizophrenia. *Archives of General Psychiatry*, 56:649.

Resnik, R. (1992). Chicken soup is poison. In E. Smith (Ed.), *Gestalt Voices*, Chapter 7. Norwood, NJ: Ablex Publishers.

Resnikoff, R. (1981). Teaching family therapy: Ten key questions for understanding the family as patient. *Journal of Marital and Family Therapy*, 7:135–142.

Resnikoff, R. (1992). Comparative therapies for an itch. In E. Smith (Ed.), *Gestalt Voices*, Chapter 25. Norwood, NJ: Ablex Publishing.

Resnikoff, R. (1995). Gestalt family therapy: An integrative influence for the varied family therapy constructs and styles of the '90s. *The Gestalt Journal*, XVIII, 2:55–75.

Resnikoff, R. & Lapidus, D. (1990). Wearing different hats as a family therapist: An integrated four-phase training model. *Acad. Psychiatry*, 14:3.

Resnikoff, R. & Lapidus, D. (1998). Psychopharmacology in conjunction with family therapy. *Journal of Family Psychotherapy*, 9(3):1–18.

Resnikoff, R., Stein, M., & Diller, L. (2000). ADHD, divorce, and parental disagreement about the diagnosis and treatment. *Developmental and Behavioral Pediatrics*, 21(1):53–57.

Rogers, C. (1961). *On Becoming a Person*. Boston, MA: Houghton Mifflin.

Rolland, J. S. (1994). *Families, Illness, and Disability: An Integrative Treatment Model*. New York: Basic Books.

Sacks, O. (1990). *The Man Who Mistook His Wife for a Hat and Other Clinical Tales*. New York: Harper & Row.

Sacks, O. (1995). *Anthropologist From Mars*. New York: Random House.

Satir, V. M. & Baldwin, M. E. (1983). *Satir: Step By Step*. Palo Alto, CA: Science and Behavior Books.

Scharff, D. E. & Scharff, J. S. (1987). *Object Relations Family Therapy*. Northvale, NJ: Jason Aronson.

Scharff, D. E. & Scharff, J. S. (1991). *Object Relations Couples Therapy*. Northvale, New Jersey: Jason Aronson.

Schwartz, J. (1995). *Brain Lock*. New York: Harper Collins.

Schwartz, C. E., Snidman, N., & Kagan, J. (1999). Adolescent social anxiety as an outcome of inhibited temperament in childhood. *J. Am. Acad. Child Adolescent Psychiatry*, Aug, 38:1008–1015.

Scotton, B., Chinen, A., & Battista, J. (Eds.) (1996). *Textbook of Transpersonal Psychiatry and Psychology*. New York: Basic Books.

Selvini-Palazzoli, M. (1986). Towards a general model of psychotic games. *Journal of Marital and Family Therapy*, 12:339–349.

Selvini-Palazzoli, M., Cecchin, G., Prata, G., & Boscolo, L. (1978). *Paradox and Counterparadox*. Northvale, NJ: Jason Aronson.

Shuchter, S. (1986). *Dimensions of Grief: Adjusting to the Death of a Spouse*. San Francisco, CA: Jossey-Bass.

Shuchter, S., Downs, N., & Zisook, S. (1996). *Biologically Informed Psychotherapy for Depression*. New York: Guilford Press.

Siever, L. & Davis, K. (1991). A psychobiological perspective on the personality disorders. *American Journal of Psychiatry*, 148(12):1647–1658.

Siever, L., New, A. S., Kirrane, R., Novotny, S., Koenigsberg, H., & Grossman, R. (1998). New biological research strategies for personality disorders. In K. Silk (Ed.), *Biology of Personality Disorders*. Washington, D.C.: American Psychiatric Press.

Solomon, M. A. (1973). A developmental, conceptual premise for family therapy. *Family Process*, June, 12(2):179–188.

Solomon, M. A. (1977). The staging of family treatment: An approach to developing the therapeutic alliance. *Journal of Marriage and Family Counseling*, April 3(2):59–66.

Stahl, S. (2000). *Essential Psychopharmacology*, 2ed. Cambridge/New York: Cambridge University Press.

Stiles, J. (1997). Hemispheric asymmetries in global and local processing-evidence from functional MRI. *Neuro Report*, 8(7):1685–1689.

Swedo, S. E., Leonard, H. L., Garvey, M., Mittleman, B., Allen, A. J., Perlmutter, S., Dow, S., Zamkoff, J., Dubbert, B. K., & Collgee, L. (1998). Pediatric autoimmune neuropsychiatric disorders associated with streptococcal infections: Clinical description of the first 50 cases. *Am. J. Psychiatry*, 155:264–271.

Swedo, S. E., Leonard, H. L., Mittleman, B. B., Allen, A. J., Rapoport, J. L., Dow, S. P., Kanter, M. E., Chapman, F., & Zabriskie, J. (1997). Identification of children with pediatric autoimmune neuropsychiatric disorders associated with streptococcal infections by a marker associated with rheumatic fever. *Am J. Psychiatry*, 154:110–112.

Swerdlow, N. (1999). Symptoms in obsessive-compulsive disorder and Tourette Syndrome: A spectrum? *CNS Spectrums*, 4(3):21–33.

Szasz, T. S. (1988). *The Myth of Psychotherapy: Mental Healing as Religion, Rhetoric, and Repression.* Syracuse, NY: Syracuse University Press.

Tomm, K. (1987). Interventive interviewing. Part I: Strategizing as a fourth guideline for the therapist. *Family Process*, 26(1):3–14.

Wachtel, E. F., & Messer, S. (1997). *Theories of Psychotherapy: Origins and Evolution* (Eds.). Washington, D.C.: American Psychological Association.

Walkup, J. T. (1999). Psychiatry of Tourette Syndrome. *CNS Spectrums*, 4(2):54–61.

Walkup, J. T. & Riddle, M. A. (1996). Tic Disorders. In: A. Tasman, J. Kay, J. A. Lieberman (Eds.), *Psychiatry*. Philadelphia, PA: W. B. Saunders (pp. 702–719).

Watzlawick, P., Weakland, J. H., & Fisch, R. (1974). *Change Principles of Problem Formation and Problem Resolution*. New York: W. W. Norton.

Wheelis, J. & Gunderson, J. (1998). A little cream and sugar: Psychotherapy with a borderline patient. *Am. J. of Psychiatry*, Jan;155:114–122.

White, M. J. & Epston, D. (1990). *Narrative Means to Therapeutic Ends*. New York: W. W. Norton.

Yehuda, R. (1998). Psychoneuroendocrinology of post-traumatic stress disorder. *Psychiatry Clinic North Am.*, June, 21(2):359–379.

Zinker, J. C. (1994). *In Search of Good Form*. San Francisco, CA: Jossey-Bass.

INDEX